Exploring Series

A FalconGuide® to Everglades National Park and the Surrounding Area

A Guide to Exploring the Great Outdoors

Roger L. Hammer

FALCONGUIDES®

GUILFORD, CONNECTICUT
HELENA, MONTANA

AN IMPRINT OF THE GLOBE PEQUOT PRESS

To buy books in quantity for corporate use
or incentives, call **(800) 962–0973**
or e-mail **premiums@GlobePequot.com**.

FALCONGUIDES®

FalconGuides is an imprint of The Globe Pequot Press.

Falcon and FalconGuides are registered trademarks of Morris Book Publishing, LLC

All photos by Roger L. Hammer

Maps by Multi Mapping Ltd. © Morris Book Publishing, LLC

ISSN 1553-9598

ISBN 978-0-7627-3432-0

Printed in the United States of America

10 9 8 7 6 5 4 3

I was able to explore strange rivers in canoes and push through tall grass to hidden mounds and stare at birds from boats. I saw things I had only heard about and learned things I could have never known.

— Marjory Stoneman Douglas,
upon publication of her book
The Everglades: River of Grass, 1947

Overview Map

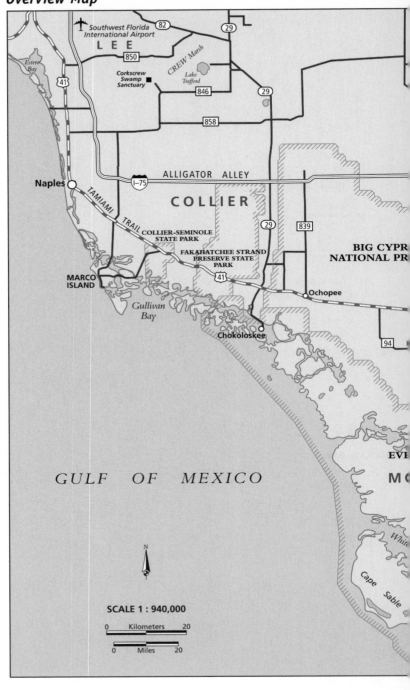

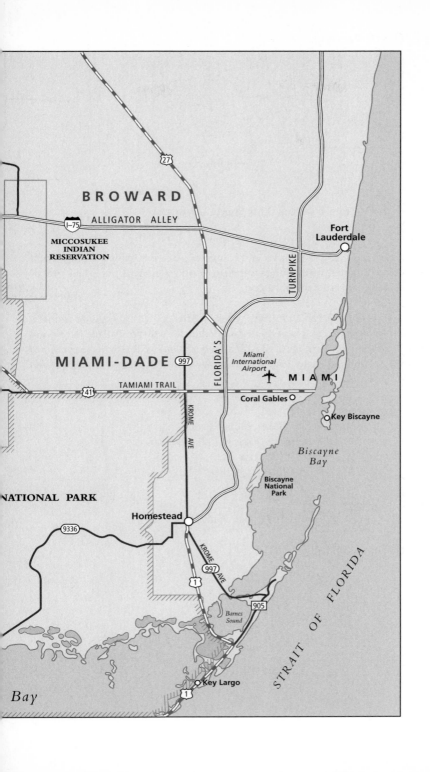

Help Us Keep This Guide Up to Date

Every effort has been made by the author and editors to make this guide as accurate and useful as possible. However, many things can change after a guide is published—regulations change, trails are rerouted, and so on.

We would love to hear from you concerning your experiences with this guide and how you feel it could be improved and kept up to date. While we may not be able to respond to all comments and suggestions, we'll take them to heart and we'll also make certain to share them with the author. Please send your comments and suggestions to the following address:

The Globe Pequot Press
Reader Response/Editorial Department
P.O. Box 480
Guilford, CT 06437

Or you may e-mail us at:
editorial@GlobePequot.com

Thanks for your input, and happy trails!

Contents

My first visit to Everglades National Park came in 1969. I drove the 38 miles from the main entrance west to Flamingo along the edge of Florida Bay. I recall having a feeling of disillusionment because the Everglades were nothing like I had expected. I envisioned the Everglades being a densely wooded and eerie swamp with orchids, ferns, and vines draping from every available tree branch. I had somehow pictured a jungle like I had seen in Tarzan movies as a child. What I found were open grassy vistas that stretched to the horizon and strange rocky pinelands that were occasionally interrupted by dense forests of broad-leaved hardwood trees. This changed rather abruptly to freshwater marsh dotted with stunted cypress trees and dome-shaped stands of taller cypress. Closer to Flamingo the landscape was overtaken by salt marsh and mangroves bordered by a muddy shoreline. Beyond that, seagrass beds stretched for miles across the shallow waters of Florida Bay.

It was only after reading *The Everglades: River of Grass* and other books about the region, coupled with many more visits, that I began to gain even the most basic understanding of this misunderstood place. Now, after more than thirty years of exploring the Everglades, I can at least comprehend the pull of the place. The Everglades creep into your inner being and make you want to return even before the sore muscles, sunburn, scrapes, and bug bites have healed. The Everglades will never be fully understood, but that is why I keep returning. I hope you will too.

When humans first began exploring the Everglades more than 1,500 years ago, the place they saw was in its primal splendor. Water flowed unimpeded through a wide, shallow vegetated marsh from Lake Okeechobee, more than 100 miles to the north, to its final destination at Biscayne Bay, Florida Bay, or the Gulf of Mexico. Wildlife was exceptionally abundant, and birds numbering in the tens of millions brightened the sky. The Everglades were intact and functional.

The natural riches of the Everglades region meant little to the first settlers and developers in Miami. They viewed the region as a vast watery hell and a frustrating hindrance to development. The foreboding swamp mocked them. This, however, would all change.

In 1905 Napoleon Bonaparte Broward was elected governor of Florida. He is who ordered the first dredge—ironically named *Everglades*—to start the slow, arduous trek from Lake Okeechobee to the sea. This was the first effort, as Governor Broward put it, to "drain the worthless swamp." In his pre-election political speeches, he pointedly proclaimed that other politicians were "draining the people and not the Everglades" and that "Yes, the Everglades is a swamp, but so was Chicago sixty years ago." In time much of the natural water flow was diverted directly into the sea and the Everglades began slowly dying. During the next sixty years, more than 90 percent of the wading birds that nested in the Everglades disappeared. The future of the Everglades was precarious at best.

On Sunday, December 6, 1947, President Harry S. Truman stood on a palmetto-thatched platform at Everglades City in the northwest corner of the Everglades and proclaimed at the end of the ceremony to 10,000 onlookers, "Here we can truly understand what the Israelitish Psalmist meant when he sang: *He maketh me to lie down in green pastures, He leadeth me beside the still waters, He restoreth my soul.*" For a moment there was unbroken silence, then applause thundered across the great swamp, the band played the national anthem, and with the stroke of a pen the Everglades became an official national treasure. It was the first national park dedicated solely for its biological wealth, culminating years of lobbying and fund-raising by a group of staunch environmentalists dedicated to making Everglades National Park a reality. Sitting in the front row during the dedication ceremony was fifty-seven-year-old author Marjory Stoneman Douglas (1890–1998), whose timeless book *The Everglades: River of Grass* had just been published.

Today's Everglades are in danger from a host of problems, including toxic levels of mercury at all levels of the food chain, pollutants from residential and agricultural areas to the north and east, disruption of natural water flow by canals, levees, and roadways, insidious urban sprawl, and invasion by alien plants and animals. In a progressive effort to repair some of the mistakes of the past, on December 11, 2000, Congress passed the Water Resources Development Act, which appropriated $7.8 billion for a twenty-five-year Everglades restoration project. This places the Florida Everglades on the threshold of great changes and gives renewed faith to those who love the place.

I thank everyone who has ever been my companion on excursions into the Everglades, whether it was a day trip to look at birds or wildflowers, a fishing excursion into the remote and beautiful backcountry, or simply sitting on Cape Sable watching the tide flow in and the sun go down. Much appreciation goes to Alan Scott, Everglades National Park Pine Island District interpreter, for commenting on a portion of the manuscript as my deadline loomed. And a heartfelt thank-you really needs to go to all of the rangers and volunteers in the various national and state parks around South Florida for their dedication and friendship. Also, a standing ovation is due to Erin Turner, executive editor of The Globe Pequot Press, and map coordinator Stefanie Ward for their much-needed assistance in the beginning stages of this book project. Professional and invaluable assistance during the final stages of this book project was cheerfully offered by managing editor Elizabeth Taylor and associate editor Jan Cronan. And thanks go to map coordinator Stephen Stringall for his attention to detail.

My purpose in writing this book is to help you find your own special places to experience on your own terms—to meditate, reflect, or simply escape from city life to be close to nature. Exploring the Everglades is a personal experience—one difficult to explain to others—and therein lies the mystery and charm of the Everglades.

The Everglades Region

Historically, the Everglades covered some 13,000 square miles from Lake Okeechobee south to the Gulf of Mexico, Florida Bay, and Biscayne Bay, literally encompassing all of southern mainland Florida. Although the Everglades are the most famous of the Florida wetlands, the predrainage Everglades were complex and included the vast Big Cypress Swamp in southwest Florida and the broad mangrove estuaries along the coastlines.

The popular term "River of Grass" oversimplifies the Everglades. They were, and still are, an interrelated ecosystem with distinct subregions, including broad prairies atop marl soils that typically were flooded only during the summer rainy season and deeper interior sloughs atop peaty soils that remained flooded in all but the driest years. Grasses and sedges dominated the true Everglades. Stretching southward along the inland edge of Biscayne Bay and then angling west into the heart of the Everglades was a wide, elevated ridge of limestone called the Miami Rock Ridge, which diverted much of the freshwater flow south and southwest through vast, open, grassy prairies. The Miami Rock Ridge was covered with seemingly endless pine forests that were occasionally interrupted by dense tropical hardwood forests called "hammocks."

When land finally gave way to the sea, the vegetation abruptly changed to coastal strand and tidal marsh behind a muddy shoreline rimmed by entangled thickets of mangroves, which sometimes reached 20 miles inland. Creeks, bays, and islands dotted the southern coast and great expanses of seagrass meadows stretched across shallow, mud-bottomed bays between mainland Florida and the rocky Florida Keys. Together these habitats formed one vast ecosystem— the Everglades.

Southern Florida's terrain is remarkably flat. Much of it is just elevated enough to be called dry land. When referring to land in southern Florida, the key word is limestone, which is mainly Miami oolite that is either at the surface or just below a thin layer of soil. Miami oolite is sedimentary limestone that filtered out of shallow seas that once covered the southern peninsula some 130,000 to 120,000 years ago. It forms jagged outcroppings called "pinnacle rock" that makes travel difficult. As flat as southern Florida is, however, it takes only a slight decline in elevation to entirely change the natural landscape from dry, rocky pineland to open marsh with plants emerging from standing water.

Elevations on the Miami Rock Ridge average only 3 to 12 feet above sea level, declining imperceptibly toward the sea. Shallow, linear depressions that cut through the Miami Rock Ridge south of present-day Miami historically allowed surface water to flow through these openings. Some of it nourished

Biscayne Bay, but most of the flow was channeled into Florida Bay to the south and the Gulf of Mexico to the west.

In the Big Cypress region, another form of limestone, the Tamiami Formation, dominates. This formation is mostly shelly limestone with shallow pockets of quartz sand.

Climate

Although southern Florida lies wholly in the temperate zone, it is closer to the equator and receives more rainfall between May and October than any other area in the continental United States. The climate is subtropical, with relatively mild, dry winters and hot, humid summers punctuated by heavy rainfall from frequent squalls and thunderstorms. Rainfall varies slightly from year to year, but the average for the southern mainland is about 60 inches annually, with most of it falling in summer. The annual rhythm of rainfall is sometimes dramatically interrupted by tropical storms and hurricanes that ply the Atlantic Ocean, the Caribbean Sea, and the Gulf of Mexico in summer and early fall. Rains can be torrential during these storms, and wind gusts can exceed 200 miles per hour.

The mean annual temperature is in the middle seventies (Fahrenheit) with summer highs in the upper eighties and low nineties and winter lows averaging in the mid-sixties. The warming effect of ocean breezes and the close proximity of the Gulf Stream that passes only a few miles offshore of the southeastern coast combine to create a favorable climate for tropical plant life. Winter frosts and even hard freezes do occasionally occur, but they are rare and seldom cause any long-term damage to native vegetation. Freezes actually define the northern limit for many Florida native plants of tropical origin. November through April marks the dry season, when water is often depleted in much of the Everglades.

Because of pleasant winter temperatures, the Everglades receive the most visitors during this season, which is unfortunate. The summer rainy season is both a time of renourishment and a time when the Everglades come alive with wildlife and wildflowers. It is only the hardy few, however, who truly appreciate summertime in the Everglades. Sweltering heat, high humidity, and insufferable swarms of the infamous Everglades mosquitoes can make life miserable, for humans and for the animals that call the Everglades home. But the Everglades need to be seen during all seasons for one to gain even the most basic understanding of the exuberant life and enchanting beauty that make this land of mystery special.

Hazards and Health Warnings

There are, as one would expect, plants and animals to be cautious of when visiting the Everglades. Three notable plants in the region have poisonous sap.

Poisonwood (Metopium toxiferum) *can be a shrub in pineland habitat or a large tree in hardwood hammocks.*

Poison ivy *(Toxicodendron radicans)* is a woody vine with three leaflets per leaf that are typically lobed but sometimes not. Simply brushing against the plant can cause a blistering skin rash on sensitive people, which usually appears after a twenty-four-hour delay. Poison ivy is especially common in the Everglades region, so care should be taken to avoid this plant.

Poisonwood *(Metopium toxiferum)* has three to seven leaflets per leaf (usually five), and these are often marked with irregular black spots. Poisonwood is a shrub in pineland habitat, but can become a large tree more than 50 feet tall in hammocks. Poisonwood can be very common along trails, especially in Everglades National Park, where there are occasional interpretive signs warning the uninformed of its toxic nature. The sap can cause a similar, but often worse, skin rash like that of the related poison ivy. The trunk of mature poisonwood trees is light brown mottled with brownish orange and often marked by black blotches where the bark has peeled away in patches. There are products available in pharmacies that can be applied both before and after contact with either of these plants. If you are particularly susceptible to poison ivy, trying these products may be useful.

Another poisonous plant in the Everglades is manchineel *(Hippomane mancinella)*, a state-listed endangered species related to the common poinsettia. Within Everglades National Park it is locally common in the coastal hammocks around Flamingo, and there are some fine specimens growing along the edge of Buttonwood Canal near Coot Bay. Boaters, canoeists, and kayakers traveling from Flamingo to the Everglades backcountry should be especially aware of this plant. The leaves have long petioles, and the leaf blades have shallow serrations

The sap of the rare, but locally common, tropical tree manchineel (Hippomane mancinella) *is very irritating to the skin, eyes, and throat.*

along the margins. The fruits are green and resemble small crab apples. The white sap is very irritating to the skin, and it can cause temporary blindness if conveyed to the eyes. Even rainwater dripping from the leaves is toxic enough to cause skin rash and burning of the eyes. The sap is water-soluble, so washing it off immediately after contact is advised. The fruits can be fatal if eaten, but some people have eaten them without effect. This, however, is ill-advised because others have suffered painful mouth, throat, and intestinal lesions.

There are four venomous snakes in southern Florida: Eastern diamondback rattlesnake, dusky pygmy rattlesnake, cottonmouth moccasin, and Eastern coral snake. The best advice is to learn what these snakes look like (see the sidebar), treat them with deserved respect, and admire them from a safe distance. The same is true if you should encounter an adult American alligator *(Alligator mississipiensis)*. Never approach alligators even if they appear to be lethargic. Alligators can lunge forward and snap their jaw and tail sideways extremely fast. They can, and do, maim and kill people. The American crocodile *(Crocodylus acutus)* also is a resident of this region, and although there has never been an encounter with humans in Florida, large American crocodiles should be given a respectful berth. They are generally shy creatures except for those that have

About Venomous Snakes in the Everglades Region

There are four venomous snakes to be aware of in South Florida. Here is how you can tell them apart from harmless snakes that inhabit the same region, along with some interesting facts about each species. If bitten, you should back away from the snake and immediately try to squeeze as much blood from the wound as possible (do not attempt to suck the venom out with your mouth), immobilize the limb, place a loose tourniquet between the bite and the torso (use a belt but be sure not to cut off blood flow to and from the limb entirely), and seek medical attention immediately. Do not attempt to kill or capture the snake because this may result in another bite (and also because even venomous snakes are protected in parks and preserves). Except for the coral snake, the bites from all other venomous snakes in Florida cause an instantaneous burning pain and eventual swelling. Lucky victims receive "dry bites," where no venom was actually injected. Bites from harmless snakes should be sterilized and treated with antibiotic ointment.

- Eastern diamondback rattlesnake *(Crotalus adamanteus):* This beautiful snake is boldly marked with a pattern of light-centered dark diamonds with yellowish borders. There is a black line across the sides of the head and a facial pit between the eye and the nostril. It is the largest venomous snake in the United States. It can reach close to 8 feet in length, but specimens more than 7 feet long are rare. So forget all the tall tales you've heard about 10-foot, and even 20-foot, rattlesnakes in Florida! If confronted, the Eastern diamondback will coil and face the intruder, usually announcing itself with a loud buzzing noise produced by the rattles at the end of its tail. If left alone, it will retreat. Being bitten is a serious medical emergency.

- Dusky pygmy rattlesnake *(Sistrurus miliarius barbouri):* This small snake is mostly brownish gray with a dorsal pattern of dark irregular markings and a bright brown stripe along its back. There are rattles at the tip of the tail, but the sound is hardly noticeable because of the small size. This snake is typically less than 2 feet in length but is very hot tempered. Being bitten is not life threatening but painful nonetheless.

The dusky pygmy rattlesnake is a common species throughout the Everglades region. Although venomous, its bite is not life threatening.

- Cottonmouth moccasin *(Agkistrodon piscivorous):* Young cottonmouths are colorfully marked with a bold pattern of dark cross bands on a brown or olive-brown body and a yellow tail. Older specimens are uniformly dark brownish black. There is a dark stripe along the side of the head and a facial pit between the eye and nostril. They are thick-bodied snakes that can reach about 5 feet in length, but they're usually much smaller. Cottonmouths are very well camouflaged, so be especially cautious when exploring areas where this snake may occur. When confronted, cottonmouths will usually hold their ground (unlike harmless water snakes). If threatened, a cottonmouth will throw its mouth wide open to reveal the mouth's white inner lining. This is a polite warning well worth heeding. These snakes will not "attack" people as is often reported by sensationalists. Being bitten is a serious medical emergency.

• Eastern coral snake *(Micrurus fulvius fulvius):* Coral snakes are boldly banded with red, yellow, and black, and the red bands are always bordered by yellow. (Harmless mimics, such as the scarlet kingsnake, have yellow and red bands separated by black.) Remember the jingle *red on yellow, kill a fellow, red on black, friend of Jack.* This is a secretive and seldom-seen snake that prefers hardwood forests, where it crawls around in the leaf litter and hunts other snakes and lizards. It must grab, hold on, and chew to introduce venom, so unless you pick one up or stand on one barefooted, there is very little chance of being bitten. The venom is neurotoxic and does not cause pain. Being bitten is a serious medical emergency.

become accustomed to people, such as those around the Flamingo marina in Everglades National Park and in some Miami-Dade County parks.

Mosquitoes can be intolerable in some areas of the park in summer and fall, especially in coastal regions where salt marsh mosquitoes flourish. Early settlers who once lived at Flamingo humorously proclaimed to newcomers that in order to talk to one another in the summer you had to throw a rock through the mosquitoes and yell through the hole! Another Everglades yarn has it that if you fall from a tree either the mosquitoes or the humidity will break your fall. Anyone who has been around Flamingo in summer can relate to that. There are numerous brands of mosquito repellent on the market, but a word of caution is in order. The active chemical ingredient in most of these products is *n-diethylmetatoluamide*, or DEET for short. Products that contain 100 percent DEET can cause severe, even fatal, allergic reactions in some people. Products that contain between 20 to 30 percent DEET are effective and safer for use. Mesh bug jackets and head screens are helpful. "Organic" products that do not contain DEET are largely ineffective when standing in the midst of summer swarms of Everglades mosquitoes, as are particular foods, diets, or electronic devices claimed by some to be effective. Running and screaming are optional! The good news is that mosquitoes are either nonexistent or reduced to tolerable levels from late fall through spring.

Repelling mosquitoes has now become an important health issue in Florida and elsewhere in the United States due to the risk of contracting West Nile virus. This mosquito-transmitted virus has proven to be fatal in some cases, especially to the elderly and those with compromised immune systems. Use common sense and do not expose yourself to mosquitoes unnecessarily. Other annoying insects in southern Florida include ticks, chiggers, sand flies (no-see-ums), deer flies, and horse flies.

There is another health warning that the reader should heed. High levels of mercury are found in many Everglades fish, especially freshwater species.

People are advised not to eat largemouth bass caught north of the main park road (which includes most of Everglades National Park as well as the Big Cypress National Preserve) more than once a week. Young children and pregnant women should avoid eating them entirely. The oscar, an exotic aquarium fish that has become established in the Everglades, has also tested high in mercury content. A mercury hot spot that backcountry fishermen should be aware of is Rookery Branch, an area northeast of Whitewater Bay that channels water flowing from the Shark River Slough to the Gulf of Mexico. The mercury level in largemouth bass, snook, and oscars is high in this region. A health warning also has been issued for spotted seatrout, gafftopsail catfish, bluefish, crevalle jack, and ladyfish caught in northern Florida Bay. Signs are posted in many areas of southern Florida to warn people of this health concern.

If you plan on fishing in saltwater, there are a few fish that can cause you physical harm. Stingrays have a defensive serrated spine near the base of the tail, and two species of saltwater catfish (hardhead and gafftopsail catfish) have sharp defensive spines on their dorsal and pectoral fins. These spines can cause excruciating pain, suffering, and possible medical emergency. Handle these with due caution. Pain-relieving antibiotic ointments are helpful. There are other fish that can cause serious bites when handled, and these include sharks, barracuda, snappers, and toadfish. Jellyfish and Portuguese Man-of-War can cause severe stings. Treat these with either ammonia or meat tenderizer that contains papain (consider bringing these items with you if you plan on swimming in water where these creatures might occur).

Puffers (blowfish) should be released and not eaten because they have internal organs that can be deadly if consumed, or if these organs are ruptured and taint the meat while the fish is being cleaned. Very large barracuda should not be consumed either because of the potential threat of ciguatera poisoning. Large predatory fish that feed on reef fish that have consumed certain species of dinoflagellates (algae) can build up toxins in their flesh. Severe cases of ciguatera poisoning can be fatal, but the toxin is most prevalent in fish that live above coral reefs, so this is not really much of a worry for fishermen in Everglades National Park. Large barracuda do, however, occur in the Gulf of Mexico.

Habitats

The Everglades are a mosaic of interdependent plant communities. Depending on the season, many of these habitats may be dry or flooded, so count on getting your feet wet if you happen to be exploring wetland habitats in the rainy season. Pine rocklands and some saw-grass prairies are characterized by sharp, exposed limestone, known locally as *pinnacle rock* or *razor rock*. Off-trail explorers in these habitats should wear appropriate shoes such as hiking boots.

Pinelands

Two types of pineland occur in the Everglades: one with an understory dominated by saw palmetto *(Serenoa repens)*, and another with a predominantly grassy understory. Soils may differ as well. Pineland habitat characterized by outcroppings of limestone on the Miami Rock Ridge is called "pine rockland," a plant community categorized as *globally imperiled* by the State of Florida. Historically, about 186,000 acres of pine rockland occurred on the Miami Rock Ridge in Miami-Dade County, but due to urbanization and agriculture, fewer than 4,000 acres remain outside of Everglades National Park. The principal upland area in Everglades National Park is Long Pine Key, which is nearly 20,000 acres of pine rockland interspersed by more than 120 tropical hardwood hammocks. Like much of the flora of southern Florida, most pine rockland plants have tropical affinities and occur no farther north in the United States than the southernmost Florida counties. Others are endemic and occur nowhere else on earth. Due to the mixture of temperate and tropical plants, pine rockland is the most floristically diverse plant community in Florida.

In contrast to the dry, rocky pinelands of the Miami Rock Ridge, the pinelands of the Big Cypress Swamp and Corkscrew Swamp differ by having moist, sandy soils and a more temperate inventory of plants.

In most southern Florida pinelands, there is a single, dominant, overstory tree, the slash pine *(Pinus elliottii)*. Beneath the tall, open, pine canopy is a highly diverse ground layer of grasses, sedges, palms, vines, woody shrubs, and herbaceous wildflowers.

Tropical Hardwood Hammocks

Hammocks are dense forests of broad-leaved hardwood trees surrounded by a contrasting plant community, usually pineland, freshwater marsh, or even mangroves. They are shady, humid forests dominated by trees of tropical origin that resemble compact islands of trees. They occur on slightly elevated locations and are usually spared from fire because of the moist, partially decayed leaf litter and humid atmosphere that creates a microclimate within the understory. They are often associated with deep solution holes carved out of the limestone that hold water during the wet season.

Cypress Swamps and Mixed-Hardwood Swamps

Cypress swamps and mixed-hardwood swamps are the dominant features of the Everglades region north of Everglades National Park. Although flooded throughout much of the year, southern Florida's swamps are typically dry in winter and spring. As water in the aquifer rises during the rainy season, it soon saturates the soil and overland flow begins.

Hardwood hammocks are among the more interesting Everglades habitats to explore.

Some cypress swamps have different configurations. Cypress "domes" are rounded forests of cypress that form around deeper water than the surrounding area. Cypress "strands" are similar except they are linear in configuration. Dwarf cypress prairie is essentially a marl prairie with stunted cypress trees growing on limestone. Some botanists separate the bald-cypress *(Taxodium distichum)* and the pond-cypress *(Taxodium ascendens)* as two distinct species. Others treat the pond-cypress as a variety of the bald-cypress. And still others regard them as the same species, citing much variation throughout their range. In this guide they will be referred to as separate species.

Mixed-hardwood swamps are characterized by cypress intermixed with a wide variety of temperate and tropical hardwood trees. In some swamps in Collier County (especially the Fakahatchee Strand) and a few hammocks of Miami-Dade County, the royal palm *(Roystonea regia)* is also common.

Freshwater Marshes

The vast stretches of freshwater marshes throughout the Everglades region can be divided into swales, marl prairies, wet prairies, and sloughs (pronounced *slews*). Everglades swales are what Marjory Stoneman Douglas referred to in her book *The Everglades: River of Grass,* and this habitat is common in much of Everglades National Park. Swales have peaty soils and are dominated by saw-grass *(Cladium jamaicense)*, but most people refer to these as *saw-grass prairies.* Saw-grass can form a vast monoculture in some areas. Marl prairies are formed above gray, claylike soils (marl) and are dominated by muhly grass *(Muhlenbergia capillaris* var. *filipes)* mixed with saw-grass and an abundance of wildflowers. Both habitats are seasonally flooded.

Wet prairies are formed atop sandy soils. This is the prairie type seen in the northern Everglades region, especially around Corkscrew Swamp. All of these shallow marshes typically drain into deeper sloughs that are flooded in all but the driest years. Some sloughs are open, sunny drainage areas, while others cut through shady, wooded swamps and are often associated with pond-apple and pop ash trees.

Although freshwater marshes may look monotonous, they are among the richest wildflower habitats in Florida. Northern visitors may find they recognize many of the marsh plants in southern Florida because, unlike most other Everglades plant communities, freshwater marshes are characterized by species of temperate origin.

Salt Marsh

Salt-marsh habitat is generally found on marl soils of coastal areas that are inundated periodically by salt or brackish water, which allows the habitat to develop where mangroves are not dense enough to create an abundance of shade. Because salt-marsh plants must be able to tolerate very salty soil, diversity within the species is lower than within other plant communities.

Mangrove Forests

Mangroves occur along Florida's muddy and rocky shorelines. They dominate the fringes of Florida Bay, Biscayne Bay, and the Gulf of Mexico in southern Florida and are an important habitat for birds and countless marine organisms. These forests are comprised of the red mangrove *(Rhizophora mangle)*, black mangrove *(Avicennia germinans)*, white mangrove *(Laguncularia racemosa)*, and buttonwood *(Conocarpus erectus)*. Mangrove forests are the most difficult of all plant communities to explore because of the arching maze of prop roots produced by red mangroves. They are also the least botanically diverse plant community in Florida, but one of the most biologically diverse, serving as critical

The arching prop roots of red mangroves make this habitat difficult to explore on foot, but the numerous creeks and rivers that wind through it make interesting canoe and kayak excursions.

habitat for an astounding number of marine organisms as well as important nesting habitat for numerous species of birds.

Beach Dunes

Its long sandy beaches make much of Florida's shoreline famous. Dune plants are hardy because they must be tolerant of dry, sandy soils, salt spray, and periodic inundation by seawater during tidal and storm surges. Natural beaches in the Everglades region occur at Cape Sable and Highland Beach in Everglades National Park; they are accessible only by boat. Key Biscayne, which is accessible by a causeway, is a barrier island between Biscayne Bay and the Straits of Florida.

How to Use This Book

This book has been written and designed to offer useful information about the various trails and wilderness adventures available to visitors of the Everglades region of southern Florida. The book covers Everglades National Park, Big Cypress National Preserve, Fakahatchee Strand Preserve State Park, Collier-Seminole State Park, Corkscrew Swamp Sanctuary, Corkscrew Regional Ecosystem Watershed (CREW) Marsh, and two Miami-Dade County parks. It includes walking and hiking trails, canoe and kayak trails and routes, and even trails for automobile and powerboat excursions. There really is something for everyone in the Everglades region. The Resources in Appendix A offer contact information for parks and preserves in southern Florida.

Some trails, especially elevated boardwalks, are easy and highly recommended for family excursions. Others are moderately difficult but can be fun and rewarding for those interested in a more challenging adventure. But there are also trails, such as the Wilderness Waterway that covers 99 miles of Everglades backcountry, that rank as either moderate or very strenuous depending on your skills as a canoeist or kayaker, and on weather and tidal conditions. Warnings about potential hazards or difficulties that you might encounter are offered in the text for each trail.

You will notice that mosquitoes and biting flies are listed as one of the special concerns for virtually every trail in this guide. Summer and fall in the Everglades region can be extremely challenging for explorers, not only because of maddening swarms of mosquitoes but due to insufferable heat and humidity as well. Most visitors, however, visit the Everglades region in late fall and winter—tourist season—when the temperature is comfortable, the mosquitoes are either nonexistent or reduced to tolerable levels, and the heat and torrential rains of summer have subsided. Admittedly, wintertime is a very good season to be exploring the Everglades, and there are many wonderful sightseeing excursions available at this time of year. But the Everglades are exciting to explore during all seasons. This book offers tips for summertime explorers too, because this is the season of high water when there is better accessibility to some backcountry areas that become dry in winter and spring. No matter what season, it is hoped that this guide helps make your trip a fun, safe, and memorable one.

Trail Chapters

Individual trail chapters are designed to help you plan your own personal wilderness adventure. Each chapter includes the following information.

Type of trail: The official uses of the trail (hiking, biking, canoeing, kayaking, or multiuse).

Type of adventure: A brief description of the type of adventure the trail offers.

Total distance: This gives you an idea of the distance of the trail, either one-way or round-trip, as well as distances between camping areas along the trail.

Nautical charts: For those trails available to canoeists and kayakers (and powerboats), this explains which nautical charts cover the region you are traveling. NOAA charts are definitely the best for navigation purposes. Some inland canoe trails are not covered by nautical charts.

Difficulty: Useful information regarding how demanding the trail or route is to traverse. Keep in mind that weather and tidal conditions can change the difficulty of some of the canoeing and kayaking trails from moderate to strenuous. Also, some of the hiking trails can change in degree of difficulty if they are flooded rather than dry. Difficulties also vary widely with the physical abilities and skills of each person.

Time required: This offers you a rough estimate of how long a reasonably fit person should take to complete the trail. This can vary greatly depending on your abilities or whether or not you wish to stop to observe wildlife, have a picnic, or just lie back and relax. Photographers, wildflower enthusiasts, and bird-watchers will take much more time than someone who is just interested in hiking and sightseeing.

Special concerns: This points out safety hazards, mosquito season, poisonous plants, dangerous animals, and trail conditions that may be of concern. Hopefully none of these special concerns will keep you from enjoying your adventure.

Scenic value: This is a subjective rating of the overall aesthetic value of the habitats visible from the trail. But remember that beauty is in the eyes of the beholder!

Overview and trail description: This is the detailed description of each trail. The information will hopefully give you some insight on what wildlife and interesting plants you might expect to see as well as some good firsthand advice from an experienced explorer of the region. Some of the human history of the area you are exploring might be offered, along with what types of fish you might try to catch if you are in the backcountry. Alternate routes might also be discussed just in case you find yourself in a predicament that you were not expecting.

Map Legend

Interstate Road	I-75
Primary Road	41
Secondary / County Road	29 94
Unimproved Road	= = = = = = = =
Hiking / Canoe Trail	- - - - - - - -
Selected Hiking / Canoe Routes	▬ ▬ ▬ ▬ ▬ ▬
Rivers / Creek	∿
Lakes	⬭
Park Boundary	▨▨▨▨▨▨
Swamps	⚘ ⚘ ⚘
Mangrove	⚘ ⚘⚘ ⚘⚘ ⚘
Airport	✈
Campground	⛺
Campsite	▲
Gate	•—•
Visitor Information	❷
Overlook	◪
Parking	🅿
Picnic	⛘
Start of Trip	START
Structure / Point of Interest	■
Towns / Cities	○

Everglades National Park, Main Entrance

The main entrance into Everglades National Park is west of Homestead and Florida City. There are ample motel accommodations and restaurants along U.S. Highway 1 and Krome Avenue (Southwest 177 Avenue; State Road 997) in both cities. There is also lodging, a marina store, and a restaurant at Flamingo along Florida Bay in Everglades National Park. Recreational vehicle (RV) and tent camping facilities are available inside the park at Long Pine Key and Flamingo. Long Pine Key and Flamingo can both be accessed from the main park road (State Road 9336).

The park's main entrance is easily accessible from the Florida Turnpike (Homestead Extension) by continuing south to its terminus at US 1 in Florida City. A sign above the off-ramp will direct you to turn right onto Palm Drive (Southwest 344 Street). Continue west to Southwest 192 Avenue (or continue west to Southwest 217 Avenue) and turn left. Proceed south to SR 9336, turn right, and continue west to the park entrance.

"Robert Is Here" fruit stand is at the corner of Palm Drive and Southwest 192 Avenue. It's a popular refreshment stop where visitors can purchase fresh local produce and enjoy tropical drinks and milk shakes. On your way to Ever-

Everglades National Park, Main Entrance

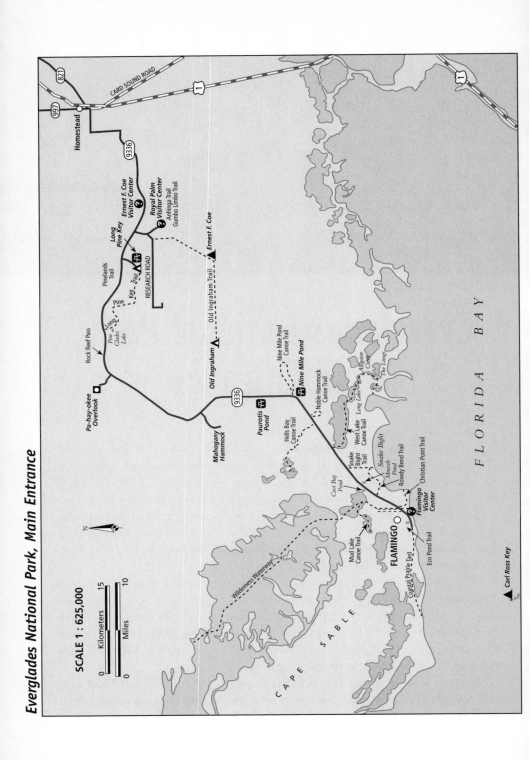

SCALE 1 : 625,000

Kilometers 15

Miles 10

glades National Park, you will also pass fields of agriculture, a mainstay of the local economy. Standard winter vegetables, such as tomatoes, sweet corn, squash, and beans, are cultivated. Due to an influx of people from tropical regions around the world, however, there are now such tropical crops as bananas, boniato, cassava, malanga, papaya, and yuca. Okra is a staple summer crop. Tropical tree crops include avocado, carambola, jackfruit, lime, longan, lychee, mamey sapote, and mango.

Ernest F. Coe Visitor Center

The Ernest F. Coe Visitor Center should be your first orientation stop at the main entrance to Everglades National Park. The hours of operation are 8:00 A.M. to 5:00 P.M. from fall through spring. Summer hours are from 9:00 A.M. to 5:00 P.M. A good visitor center should beckon you to go explore the outdoors, and this center does just that. Here you will find opportunities to learn about the Everglades through static and interactive interpretive displays, through educational videos, and from park rangers and volunteers at the front desk. A free brochure map of the park is available in English, Spanish, French, Italian, or German. Other informational handouts in various languages are also available upon request. For adventurous travelers who want to get off the beaten path, there is a free map called Hiking and Biking Trails of Long Pine Key available by request at the front desk and at the entrance station. This map shows all of the old firebreak roads that traverse Long Pine Key, and these trails are excellent for both hiking and biking.

There is also a well-stocked bookstore and gift shop inside the Ernest F. Coe Visitor Center that offers many fine field guides and other educational books on the Everglades and surrounding areas. Other FalconGuides sold here include *Hiking Florida, Everglades Wildflowers,* and *Florida Keys Wildflowers.* Guided walks, canoe trips, and boat tours are available in some areas of the park. Daily schedules can be obtained at the Ernest F. Coe Visitor Center, Royal Palm Visitor Center, or Flamingo Visitor Center, all accessible from the main entrance.

Distances from the Ernest F. Coe Visitor Center to areas outside the park:

Homestead	11 miles (18 km)
Miami International Airport	45 miles (72 km)
Key West	135 miles (217 km)

About Ernest F. Coe

No other person was more dedicated to making Everglades National Park a reality than Ernest F. Coe (1866–1951). He and other staunch environmentalists of the time, including little-known author Marjory Stoneman Douglas (1890–1998), worked tirelessly to help save what was being deemed "a worthless swamp" by developers and politicians. Their efforts were rewarded in December 1947 when Pres. Harry S. Truman (1884–1972) dedicated the park in front of 10,000 onlookers. Ernest F. Coe was reluctantly sitting next to the president after being persuaded into attending the event by friends and colleagues. His reluctance to attend the ceremony stemmed from the park's boundaries being drastically reduced in size from what he had envisioned. Coe wanted the park to encompass the area from the southern edge of Lake Okeechobee not only to include the Big Cypress Swamp but the Upper Florida Keys as well. The boundaries agreed upon by politicians angered Coe, and he threatened to boycott the dedication. In retrospect, had Ernest Coe's vision become reality, the Everglades system would not be in the trouble it is today. By not including the area between the Big Cypress Swamp and Lake Okeechobee, politicians allowed what has been likened to owning the garden hose but not the faucet. Supported by import tariffs, Big Sugar, a controversial industry that cultivates thousands of acres of sugarcane in the rich muck south of Lake Okeechobee, has negatively altered the quantity and quality of water that reaches the Everglades. And this is one of the principal reasons why Everglades National Park has been deemed one of the most endangered parks in the nation. Without water there can be no Everglades. Ernest F. Coe was, indeed, a true visionary. Today Everglades National Park is also a designated World Biosphere Reserve and a Wetland of International Importance.

Entrance Fees

As you leave the Ernest F. Coe Visitor Center, the entrance station straddles the main park road. The current fee at the main entrance of Everglades National Park is $10 per private vehicle; your receipt allows entry for seven consecutive days. Another option is to purchase an Everglades National Park Pass ($25), which allows free admission into all entrances of Everglades National Park for one year. The pass holder must be in the vehicle in order for a pass to be honored. There is an additional $5.00 fee for entering the park by vehicle with a motorized boat and an additional $3.00 fee for a nonmotorized vessel, such as a canoe or kayak. This fee is charged whether or not you actually plan on using

Ernest F. Coe Visitor Center at the main entrance to Everglades National Park should be your first orientation stop.

the vessel in the park. Those who frequently trailer boats into the park can purchase an annual pass for $60. Pedestrians, bicyclists, and motorcyclists are charged a $5.00 per person entrance fee. There is no fee for visitors entering the park by boat. Be advised that all motorized vessels in Florida must have proper registration and safety equipment, which includes canoes powered by small outboard motors.

The National Park Service also offers a National Park Pass ($50), which allows free admission for one calendar year from the date of purchase into any national park that charges a fee. And you can purchase a Golden Eagle Hologram ($15) that, when affixed to your National Park Pass, allows free admission for one calendar year into any national park, U.S. Fish and Wildlife Preserve, or U.S. Monument. Seniors (62 years of age or older) who are U.S. citizens pay a one-time fee of $10 to acquire a Golden Age Pass, which allows free lifetime admission into any U.S. national park, preserve, or monument. A Golden Access Passport is available for free to all U.S. citizens or residents with lifetime disabilities.

Bona fide educational groups that are not being led by a paid guide may qualify for an entrance-fee waiver. You can request a waiver by writing to the Chief Ranger's Office (Everglades National Park, 40001 State Road 9336, Homestead, FL 33034).

Backcountry campers must pay a $10.00 permit fee (per group) plus a $2.00 per-person, per-day camping fee. Land-based campsites accessible by hiking (including Long Pine Key and Flamingo campgrounds) are $14.00 per night, or $7.00 per night for Golden Age Pass and Golden Access Passport holders. Stay limits are fourteen days during the winter season and thirty days in a calendar year. For detailed information on camping in Everglades National Park campgrounds, obtain a copy of the campground rules and regulations at any visitor center, entrance station, or campground.

The main entrance to Everglades National Park is open 24 hours a day, 365 days a year.

Permitted Activities

Hiking, biking, boating, canoeing, kayaking, wind surfing, camping, fishing, and photography are all permitted recreational activities within Everglades National Park. Camping and fishing are restricted to specified areas within the park. Check at the ranger stations for details regarding camping and fishing opportunities. Off-trail hiking (but not biking) is also allowed, but use your common sense. Take a compass or hand-held GPS (Global Positioning System) to avoid getting lost, and learn which hazards you might encounter (poisonous plants, venomous snakes, dangerous animals). Large groups should obey environmental ethics and remain on designated trails to avoid creating trampled areas in pristine natural areas. An educational and safe way to enjoy off-trail exploring is to join one of the ranger-guided walks, some of which include wading into cypress domes and other wetland habitats. Ranger-guided canoe trips are also available for a fee.

Collecting seashells is permitted as long as the shells are unoccupied (hermit crabs use shells as homes). One quart of shells per person per day is allowed.

Prohibited and Restricted Activities

Personal watercraft (also called "Jet Skis" or "wet bikes"), waterskiing, airboats, all-terrain vehicles (ATVs), off-trail biking, firearms, spearfishing, commercial fishing, and hunting are all prohibited within Everglades National Park. Airboat rides are currently available from private commercial enterprises located east of the main park entrance in Florida City and along Tamiami Trail (U.S. Highway 41), mostly within the Miccosukee Indian Reservation. Be advised, however, that airboats are loud, environmentally detrimental, and potentially dangerous. A more educational and relaxing way to enjoy the Everglades region is by foot, bicycle, motorized boat, canoe, or kayak.

Dogs are prohibited along trails but are allowed in parking lots and camp-grounds, although they must be restrained on a leash at all times (*never* allow a dog to approach areas where alligators reside). Horses are currently allowed along designated trails of Long Pine Key. Smoking is prohibited on all trails.

Be especially aware that feeding wildlife, especially alligators, is prohibited and can result in a fine. If alligators become accustomed to a food source, they lose their fear and purposely approach people for handouts. This is not only a safety risk to you, because adult alligators do attack and sometimes kill people (and dogs), but also to the alligators, because once an alligator begins to habit-ually approach people, it is trapped and destroyed. Therefore, by illegally feed-ing an alligator, you pose a threat to yourself and to the well-being of the alligator.

Campfires are allowed only below the high-tide line on specified beaches (prohibited at all other campsites, including land-based sites). Portable motors (generators, chain saws) are prohibited at all wilderness campsites.

Collecting plants, including air plants that have fallen to the ground, is pro-hibited without special research permits. Parks and preserves sometimes harbor

rare plants, some of which are on the verge of extinction, so removing even a single individual, or picking a flower, can be catastrophic to a popula-tion. Admire their beauty and leave them where you found them, both for the benefit of the plant and future explorers like yourself. Collecting driftwood, sea horses, starfish, conch, tropical fish, lobster, coral, and sponges is also prohibited.

The playing of recorded birdcalls within the park is not allowed. Birders sometimes play record-ings of calls to help bring birds into view for obser-vation. This sometimes works too well, as evidenced by a man who played a taped call of a barred owl while on the Mahogany Hammock boardwalk in Everglades National Park. A resident barred owl in the hammock took offense to the "intruder owl" in its territory and attacked the man holding the recorder, leaving deep talon wounds in his face. Playing taped calls also disrupts the normal activi-ties of birds.

Also, *do not exceed posted speed limits*, both for your safety and for the benefit of wildlife in the park. Panther crossing signs are posted in areas where Florida panthers are known to cross road-ways. The small population of this critically imper-

Florida panther crossing signs are posted wherever this feder-ally endangered animal is known to cross roadways. Slow down and remain alert when you see these signs.

iled, federally listed endangered mammal suffers more from road kills than any other threat. Law-enforcement rangers are in vehicles equipped with radar, and they often monitor the speed of vehicles throughout the park. Slow down, relax, and enjoy the scenery.

Closed Areas

Closed areas represent less than 1 percent of the total area of Everglades National Park. Some areas may be temporarily closed in the event of fire, whether it is a wildfire or a prescribed burn being conducted by resource managers. Some areas may be closed periodically for restoration or research monitoring, and some facilities and boardwalks within the park may also be temporarily closed for refurbishing. At present Chekika Recreation Area in Everglades National Park is closed and may not reopen due to expected flooding associated with the Everglades Restoration Project currently under way.

There is one portion of northeast Florida Bay that is permanently closed because it is deemed to be critical nesting habitat for the American crocodile. This area begins about 17 miles east of Flamingo and includes Little Madeira Bay, Taylor River, East Creek, Mud Creek, Mud Bay, Davis Creek, Joe Bay, Snag Bay, and the interior bays from the northern shore of Long Sound to US 1. The area is clearly posted by signs located offshore, so do not enter this area for any reason. It is marked in pink on the free Everglades National Park map and brochure available from ranger stations.

Most keys and beaches in Florida Bay are closed to the public, with the exception of designated campsites on Carl Ross Key, Little Rabbit Key, and North Nest Key. Bradley Key, just offshore of Flamingo, is open only during daylight hours. Access is allowed only on the northern beach of Pavilion Key, which is located about 7 miles south of Chokoloskee Island in the Ten Thousand Islands. The remainder of the key is closed. For a detailed listing of closed areas for boaters, consult the free pamphlet *Everglades Boating Regulations*, available at all visitor centers and entrance stations. Other areas can be posted by executive order of the park superintendent.

The entire park may be closed to all entry during a hurricane. Campers, visitors, and boaters throughout the park may be ordered to vacate if a hurricane is imminent. Visitors in South Florida during the summer and fall should pay close attention to daily weather reports. A Hurricane Watch is issued if hurricane force winds (74-plus mph) are expected within the next thirty-six hours, and a Hurricane Warning goes into effect if the storm can make landfall within twenty-four hours. Ample warning is given so, for your safety, it is highly recommended that you evacuate South Florida if a hurricane is approaching. Hurricane Andrew devastated this region with 165 mph sustained winds (gusting to more than 200 mph) on August 24, 1992. It caused 51 deaths, left 175,000 people homeless, caused more than $20 billion in damages, and knocked out electrical power and telephone service to 1.3 million homes and businesses for many weeks. Andrew was one of only three Category 5 hurricanes to hit the United States since 1900. Hurricanes should not be taken lightly. Evidence of Hurricane Andrew is still visible in Everglades National Park, especially by the twisted, fallen, and broken pine trees throughout Long Pine Key and the huge toppled trees along the Mahogany Hammock boardwalk. A free twelve-minute video about the effects of Hurricane Andrew is available for viewing at the Ernest F. Coe Visitor Center upon request.

Boat Ramps

Boat ramps within Everglades National Park are located at Flamingo, Little Blackwater Sound south of Florida City on US 1, and West Lake east of Flamingo. Commercial ramps are also available in Everglades City and Chokoloskee Island on the west coast.

Motor Restrictions

Some areas within Everglades National Park are accessible only by canoe or kayak. For a complete listing of these areas, refer to the free pamphlet *Everglades Boating Regulations*, available at any visitor center or entrance station. Watercraft with outboard motors of 6 horsepower or less are allowed in West Lake but not beyond.

No-Wake Zones and Boating Etiquette

Propeller damage to sea-grass beds is detrimental to the marine environment, so boaters in shallow waters should be conscientious and use a push pole or paddles when necessary. No-wake zones are posted in many areas, either for the safety of canoeists and kayakers or for the well-being of West Indian manatees. In the Flamingo area, no-wake zones are posted in both boat basins, Buttonwood Canal, Tarpon Creek, Avocado Creek, North Prong creeks, and East Cape Canal. In the Everglades City area, there are no-wake zones in Alligator Creek, Plate Creek, Halfway Creek, and between Markers 86 and 87 along the Wilderness Waterway. In the Key Largo area, no-wake zones are posted in Marker 42 Creek, the Boggies, Shell Creek, McCormick Creek, and around Nest Key. For safety and courtesy always slow down to a no-wake speed when approaching or passing canoes, kayaks, anchored boats, or fishermen in boats not under power.

Fishing Regulations

Be sure to pick up a copy of the free pamphlet *Everglades Fishing Regulations* from any visitor center or entrance station if you plan to try your luck fishing within Everglades National Park. This pamphlet is a supplement to the Florida

Saltwater Recreational Fishing Regulations set by the state. Fishing regulations within Everglades National Park are sometimes stricter than state regulations, especially regarding possession limits, so make certain that you are fully informed before wetting a line. State regulations change frequently as well, so be sure you are up-to-date with the latest size and possession limits, and that you are aware of closed seasons. Some species, such as goliath grouper (jewfish) and sawfish, are fully protected and illegal to harvest at any time.

A special stamp ($2.00 each) affixed to the license is required to harvest either spiny lobster (crawfish) or snook in Florida, but note that it is illegal to harvest spiny lobster within Everglades National Park and in Biscayne Bay within Biscayne National Park. Recreational freshwater fishing requires a license for persons age sixteen through sixty-four except when using a cane pole or hand line in your county of residence. Florida residents can purchase a combination license for both freshwater and saltwater recreational fishing, or they may purchase a lifetime license (which includes a snook and crawfish stamp). All anglers may purchase licenses using a credit card by phoning (888) FISH FLORIDA (888–347–4356) toll-free, or they may inquire at any county tax collector's office. Many sporting-goods stores, bait-and-tackle shops, and other retail outlets that sell hunting and fishing equipment also sell licenses. For detailed information on fishing-license requirements and Florida fishing regulations, visit the Florida Fish and Wildlife Conservation Commission Web site at www.floridafisheries.com.

Professional fishing guides offer personalized guided fishing trips into Everglades National Park, and the half-day or full-day charter fee often includes a temporary fishing license for out-of-state visitors. For information on fishing-guide services in Florida, visit www.FLFishingCharters.com or inquire at the Flamingo Visitor Center or Gulf Coast Visitor Center in Everglades National Park.

Canoeing the Everglades Backcountry

Canoeists (and kayakers) can enjoy hours—even days or weeks—exploring the backcountry waters of Everglades National Park. The 99-mile Wilderness Waterway, which connects Everglades City and Chokoloskee Island at the northwest corner of the park to Flamingo along Florida Bay to the south, is one of the last real wilderness adventures left in Florida (see Appendix F: Wilderness Waterway Campsite Information). All, or part, of the Wilderness Waterway can be a rewarding—although sometimes challenging—experience for anyone who enjoys wilderness adventure in a canoe or kayak. But use common sense and never embark on trips that may be beyond your physical abilities or skills. There are many less-challenging destinations in Everglades National Park. To keep any boating adventure safe and enjoyable, see the Canoe Safety Tips and Canoe Comfort Tips in the Appendix.

Royal Palm Hammock

The turnoff to Royal Palm Hammock is a little more than a mile from the entrance station and is marked by signage. But on your way to the Royal Palm Hammock turnoff, you may want to stop at the Taylor Slough Bridge to see what sort of wildlife and wildflowers are present. In the fall months an interesting native orchid, the scented ladies' tresses *(Spiranthes odorata)*, flowers right along the edge of the road swale near the Taylor Slough Bridge. The attractive white flowers are on an erect spike, often in standing water, so expect to get your feet wet if you want to take in their delightful fragrance. Also look for alligators, interesting fish, frogs, snakes, and wading birds in and around the deeper channel that flows under the bridge. Watch for common yellowthroats, red-winged blackbirds, and occasional night herons in the willow thickets near the bridge.

Royal Palm Hammock is located a few miles south of the main park road. Ranger-led walks and talks are conducted here. The times they're held are posted outside the Royal Palm Visitor Center. The visitor center includes a small bookstore and has restrooms, and vending machines are outside. A seating area is available on the south side of the visitor center, where interpretive talks are conducted by rangers. This area gets its name from the royal palm *(Roystonea regia)*, a tall majestic palm that is native to Florida. Early explorers and botanists used these towering royal palms as landmarks to find Royal Palm Hammock long before there were trails or roads leading into the Everglades. Look closely on the trunks of the royal palms for the bark mantis. This relative of the praying mantis is two-toned gray and is well camouflaged against the gray lichens that cover the palm trunks.

There are three trails accessible from this location: Anhinga Trail, Gumbo Limbo Trail, and Old Ingraham Trail. This area was once the location of Royal Palm State Park, dedicated on November 22, 1916, which was incorporated into Everglades National Park in 1947.

When you arrive at the parking lot of Royal Palm Hammock, make sure you secure any food items, or you will likely find some very fat and happy crows around your vehicle when you return. Don't be surprised if the crows hop up on your front fender when you arrive and dine on the insects stuck to your radiator screen. The trees in the parking-lot island are West Indian mahogany *(Swietenia mahagoni),* and you may notice their large woody brown fruits that split open and release winged seeds that spiral in the air. You should be able to find parts of split fruits on the ground beneath the trees. Look for warblers in their canopy anytime from fall into spring.

Also, just as a precaution, put any valuables in your trunk before heading out on your adventure.

Anhinga Trail

TYPE OF TRAIL: Walking.

TYPE OF ADVENTURE: Walk on a paved walkway and elevated boardwalk over a freshwater marsh (Taylor Slough).

TOTAL DISTANCE: 0.75 mile.

DIFFICULTY: Easy. Wheelchair accessible.

TIME REQUIRED: 1 to 2 hours or more.

SPECIAL CONCERNS: Not much shade, so dress appropriately. Alligators sometimes rest very close to (or even on) the trail, so keep a safe distance even if they appear to be lethargic. For safety do not allow children to stand on the low barrier wall or the wood railing along the trail. Even in summer mosquitoes are usually tolerable along this trail during the daytime.

SCENIC VALUE: Outstanding. This is a classic Everglades freshwater marsh with opportunities to observe resident and seasonal birds, reptiles, amphibians, fish, and diverse freshwater wetland plants.

OVERVIEW AND TRAIL DESCRIPTIONS: The trailhead is located next to the visitor center. This is one of the most popular trails in all of Everglades National Park, so bring your camera, binoculars, and field guides. This is also where visitors often get their very first look at an American alligator in its natural habitat, and it is a very popular birding spot as well. Winter and spring are the best seasons to see an abundance of wildlife because they mark the dry season, which causes fish to become concentrated in permanently flooded areas like Taylor Slough. The fish, in turn, attract birds, alligators, and other animals that come to feast on the bounty. There is usually an abundance of birds along the trail, and most can be viewed at relatively close range because they are accustomed to pedestrians. Double-crested cormorants and the trademark anhingas often perch on the low fence adjacent to the trail, allowing viewing at just a few feet away. Wood storks, herons, egrets, and moorhens are common sights. Anhingas nest in trees around the boardwalk, and their nesting activities can be seen from January into early summer. You may see alligators positioned beneath the nests as they wait for a hapless nestling to fall. Young anhingas are white and fluffy and have pinkish feet, unlike either of their parents.

Be prepared for the unexpected anytime you are exploring in the Everglades. In January 2003 an alligator attacked a huge Burmese python that swam across Taylor Slough, keeping the snake in its jaws for twenty-four hours until being challenged for the prize by a larger alligator. The snake escaped during the ensuing battle between the two alligators, much to the amazement of the

Watchable wildlife: An anhinga perches on the railing along Anhinga Trail in Ever-glades National Park, seemingly oblivious to passersby.

As water levels drop in fall, American alligators congregate in deeper areas such as Taylor Slough.

crowd of onlookers. Although Burmese pythons are supposed to be in Asia, not the Everglades, this incident exemplifies why the Everglades can be a very exciting place to explore.

Specialty birds to look for here include purple gallinules, glossy ibis, wood storks, limpkins, and American bitterns. Short-tailed hawks, Swainson's hawks, red-tailed hawks, swallow-tailed kites, and even bald eagles sometimes soar overhead with vultures. Turtles, snakes, and the occasional river otter also can be seen around Taylor Slough. A menagerie of exotic (nonnative) fish can be seen here as well, including walking catfish and a number of species of cichlids, which now share the Everglades with such native fish as largemouth bass, bluegill, spotted gar, and mosquitofish. Listen for the deep, throaty grunts of the pig frog in spring and summer, and the eerie primal growling of mature alligators as nesting season approaches. The vibration created by a growling alligator causes the water over its back to jump about. When spring and summer rains begin, a loud chorus of frogs can erupt all at once, especially at dusk. Common species include green tree frogs, cricket frogs, little grass frogs, and pig frogs. Listen also for the sheeplike bleats of southeastern narrowmouth toads. If the mosquitoes aren't too bad, hang around for the entertainment. Also around dusk you may hear the plaintive wailing of limpkins. The call of this wading bird has been described as one of the weirdest sounds of nature, reminiscent of a wailing child.

Some of the flowering native plants that are easily visible along this trail include string-lily *(Crinum americanum)*, oceanblue morning-glory *(Ipomoea indica* var. *acuminata)*, buttonbush *(Cephalanthus occidentalis)*, arrowhead *(Sagittaria lancifolia)*, and pickerelweed *(Pontederia cordata)*. Take your time and enjoy the show of wildlife and wildflowers along this trail.

Buttonbush (Cephalanthus occidentalis) *is a common shrub in wet habitats throughout the Everglades region and is especially common along the Anhinga Trail in Everglades National Park.*

Gumbo Limbo Trail

TYPE OF TRAIL: Walking.

TYPE OF ADVENTURE: Short walk on a paved trail through Royal Palm Hammock.

TOTAL DISTANCE: 0.5 mile.

DIFFICULTY: Easy. Wheelchair accessible.

TIME REQUIRED: One-half to 1 hour.

SPECIAL CONCERNS: Mosquitoes and biting flies in summer and fall.

SCENIC VALUE: Good. This is a mature tropical hardwood hammock with numerous species of native tropical trees and associated birds and other wildlife.

ABOUT THE GUMBO-LIMBO

The gumbo-limbo is one of the most interesting trees of the Everglades region. Any piece of a trunk or branch will root if placed in the ground, giving rise to the name "living fencepost" in parts of its native range. Even when a gumbo-limbo is toppled by storm winds, the roots that face upward simply sprout leaves and grow into trees. The thin bark allows the tree to photosynthesize through the trunk and branches in the dappled light of hammocks, and this trait is especially useful when the tree is leafless in late winter and spring. Peeling bark also allows the tree to shed epiphytic plants off of the trunk and branches. Even though epiphytes do not harm the tree in any way, they do trap nutrients.

Now-extinct Calusa Indians in southwestern Florida once used the sap of the tree as a source of birdlime. Birdlime is sticky tree sap smeared on branches to entrap birds that land on it. Calusa Indians trapped native songbirds (mostly mockingbirds and cardinals) in this manner, then put them in makeshift cages and took them in canoes (some up to 40 feet long) to Cuba to trade for tobacco and other goods.

When African slaves were brought to Florida decades later, some of them learned of the use of the gumbo-limbo as a source of birdlime and used the sap to trap birds for food and trade. Some of these Africans were from the Bantu tribe who were adept at using birdlime in their homeland. The Bantu name for the tree became *nkômbô edimbu* (translating to "runaway slave's birdlime"), and the name was modified in English as "gumbo-limbo" over time.

Settlers even once used the straight trunks of young gumbo-limbo trees to pen West Indian manatees. The wood is light and floats in seawater, so bundles of the trunks could be floated into the shallows and shoved into the soft mud of Florida Bay to make corrals. West Indian manatees, or "sea cows," were kept penned as a source of food, much like cattle. Today these areas are still indicated on nautical charts as the Cow Pens. The sap of gumbo-limbo also has been used as an ingredient in varnish; the wood has been carved into merry-go-round horses; and the fruits are a favorite food of flycatchers (especially kingbirds) in southern Florida. The comical name "tourist tree" relates to the red peeling bark that resembles the skin of a sunburned tourist. Other names are gum-elemi and West Indian birch.

OVERVIEW AND TRAIL DESCRIPTION: The trailhead is located on the south side of the visitor center. About 85 percent of the trees in the hammocks of Everglades National Park are of tropical origin, and this trail is named for the gumbo-limbo (*Bursera simaruba*), a tropical tree characterized by thin, red peeling bark.

They are easily recognized along the trail. This is also an excellent trail to look for warblers and other birds during fall and spring migration. Keep an eye and ear out for vireos, flycatchers, gnatcatchers, cuckoos, and other resident or seasonal birds that inhabit hardwood forests. You can also see some interesting epiphytes—ferns, orchids, and bromeliads—by closely scrutinizing the trunks and branches of trees, especially rough-barked species such as live oak *(Quercus virginiana).*

Old Ingraham Trail

TYPE OF TRAIL: Hiking, biking, and tent camping.

TYPE OF ADVENTURE: Hike or bike on an unpaved historic roadway. Tent camping by permit allowed at two designated areas along the trail.

TOTAL DISTANCE: 22 miles round-trip from Royal Palm Hammock and back.

DIFFICULTY: Moderate.

TIME REQUIRED: A half day or more by bike; all-day hike. Two campsites are available along the trail for hikers or bikers who do not want to make the round-trip in a single day.

SPECIAL CONCERNS: Mosquitoes and biting flies in summer and fall. Large alligators sometimes bask on the trail. No facilities.

SCENIC VALUE: Excellent. The trail traverses a variety of habits with occasional open vistas of the Everglades.

OVERVIEW AND TRAIL DESCRIPTION: Historic Old Ingraham Trail can be accessed off of Gumbo Limbo Trail or at the southwest corner of the cleared area near the parking lot of Royal Palm Hammock. It was once the road that led to Flamingo but was closed after the new main park road was completed. Old Ingraham Trail is not marked by signage, but it offers good birding opportunities as it bisects various habitats. It is a wide trail that is excellent for hiking or biking, and because it is seldom traveled, it is especially nice for those seeking solitude. Near the beginning of the trail, visitors may notice exotic (nonnative) bromeliads, ferns, and other plants growing among the native vegetation. Members of a Women's Garden Club purposely planted these back when this area was a state park. Even residents in South Florida at the time regarded the Everglades as rather bland and boring, so the consensus was that exotic plants were necessary to make the area more interesting and colorful for visiting tourists. Some of these species are being left for their historical value, but many others have been eradicated because of their invasive tendencies.

Old Ingraham Trail runs south-southwest for about 6 miles and then turns

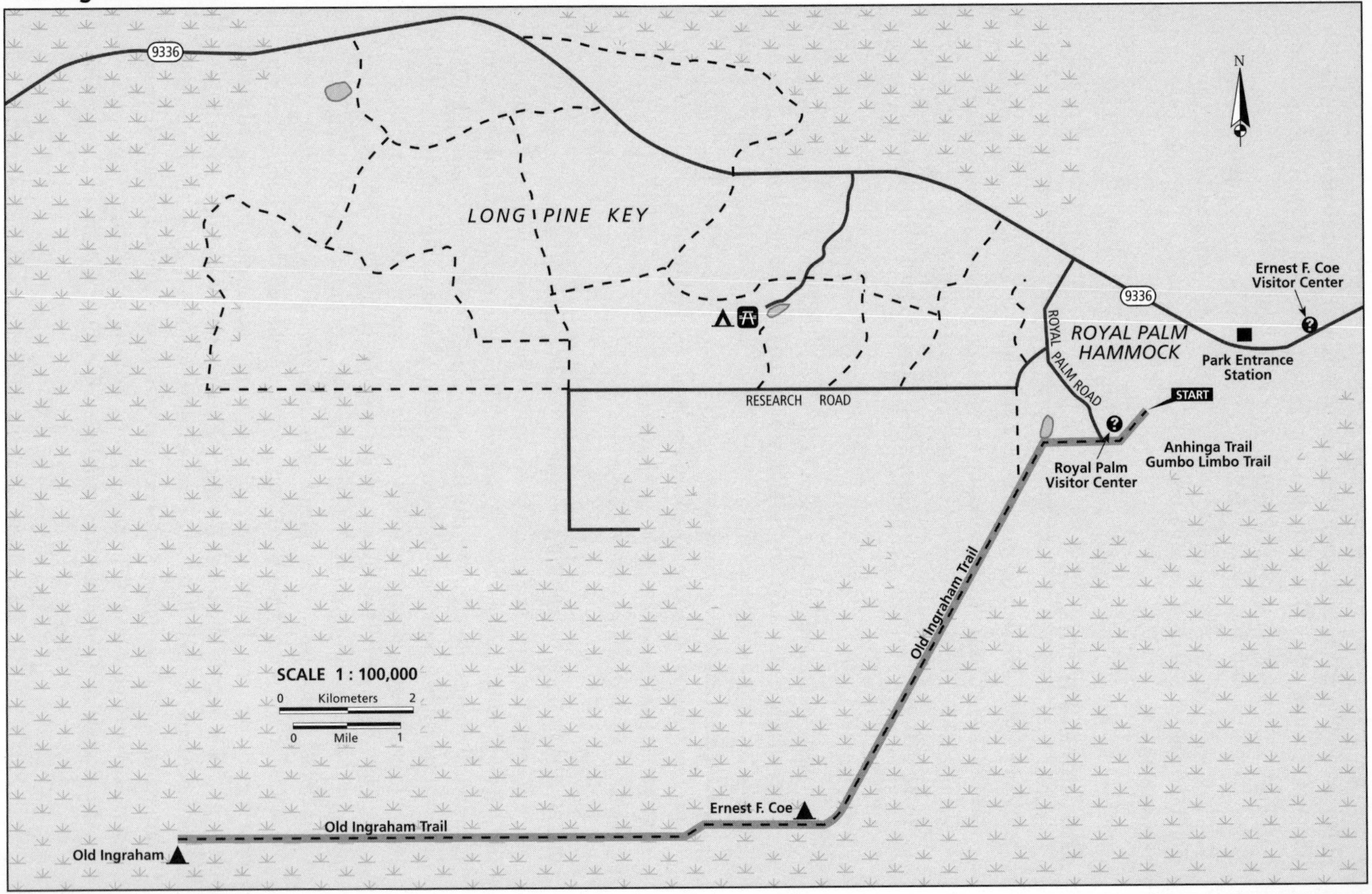

Old Ingraham Trail

SCALE 1 : 100,000

Kilometers 0 ... 2

Mile 0 ... 1

N

Ernest F. Coe
Visitor Center

Park Entrance
Station

9936

ROYAL PALM HAMMOCK

ROYAL PALM ROAD

START

Anhinga Trail
Gumbo Limbo Trail

Royal Palm
Visitor Center

Old Ingraham Trail

Ernest F. Coe

LONG PINE KEY

RESEARCH ROAD

9936

Old Ingraham Trail

Old Ingraham

due west. The Ernest F. Coe campsite is 6 miles from the trailhead at Royal Palm Hammock, and the Old Ingraham campsite is 5 miles past the Ernest F. Coe campsite. A required backcountry camping permit can be obtained at the main entrance station.

Research Road—Hole-in-the-Donut

Midway between the main park road and Royal Palm Hammock is a paved road that leads west to the Daniel Beard Research Center and to an area of abandoned agricultural land called the Hole-in-the-Donut. The agricultural land was abandoned in the 1970s after the National Park Service deemed it to be inappropriate for commercial agriculture to be continued within the boundaries of Everglades National Park. The area quickly became infested with exotic pest plants, mostly Brazilian pepper *(Schinus terebinthifolius)*, a large aggressive shrub from South America, and shoebutton ardisia *(Ardisia elliptica)*, an invasive shrub from tropical Asia. These two species formed a near monoculture across hundreds of acres.

In order to reclaim the disturbed land, the park began an ambitious project to clear the land and then scrape it down below grade to allow flooding in the rainy season. Native freshwater wetland plants moved in and the area is now recovering. It has quickly become one of the best places to see white-tailed deer, waterfowl, and other resident and seasonal wildlife. Most of the accumulated fill that resulted from scraping the area below grade was used to create large elevated pads, which have been overtaken by native vegetation. In the wet season this elevated land offers refuge for small herds of white-tailed deer, so it is always a good idea to scan the land with binoculars or spotting scopes from the road.

This road turns south just past the Daniel Beard Research Center and then turns back east, where it terminates at an old abandoned missile site established during the Cuban missile crisis, which had the potential of starting World War III. The Soviet Union was placing missiles in Cuba, just 90 miles from the United States, so Pres. John F. Kennedy placed a military ship blockade around Cuba, which created a standoff. The Soviet Union ended up removing the missile bases from Cuba. Everglades National Park is now making plans to develop this abandoned Cold War–relic missile site as an educational interpretive site for park visitors. As of this writing, the project is still in its development stages.

Long Pine Key

As you travel west on the main park road, Long Pine Key is the first turnoff after Royal Palm Hammock. Long Pine Key is the principal upland area of Everglades National Park and encompasses about 20,000 acres of pine rockland

Long Pine Key in Everglades National Park is mostly covered by pine rockland, a habitat listed as globally imperiled by the State of Florida.

habitat interspersed with more than 120 tropical hardwood hammocks. Long Pine Key is periodically bisected by wide swaths of Everglades prairie, often called *finger glades*, through which water flows during the wet season. The word *key* in Florida, and *cay* in the Bahamas (pronounced "key" or "kay"), originally came from *cairi*, a Lucayan word for "island." The Lucayans were an Arawak Indian tribe from the Bahamas. This is also the origin of the Spanish *cayo*, which translates to "a small, low-lying island." This word aptly fits Long Pine Key, a low-lying island surrounded by water throughout most of the year.

The Long Pine Key turnoff leads visitors to a campground, picnic area, and restrooms. It is also an access road to some good hiking and biking trails. The campground can accommodate both recreational vehicles and tent campers. Reservations are highly recommended during the peak season from fall through winter. Campsites are available on a first-come basis, but reservations can be made up to five months in advance by phoning the National Parks Reservation System at (800) 365–2267 or by visiting www.reservations.nps.gov.

There is a lake bordering the campground and picnic area (swimming prohibited; fishing allowed) that was dredged for fill to create the main park road. On your way to the campground area on Long Pine Key, you will pass gated firebreaks on the left and right that are available as hiking or biking trails (the trail heading east is available only to hikers; the trail heading west is also available to bikers).

Gate 3 Firebreak Trail

TYPE OF TRAIL: Hiking.

TYPE OF ADVENTURE: Hike along a graded firebreak that traverses pine rockland and prairie habitat.

TOTAL DISTANCE: 2 miles one way to Research Road at Gate 2A; 3 miles one way to Research Road at Gate 2; 4-mile loop from the trailhead to Gate 2A, then west on Research Road to Gate 2B, and then north to the Long Pine Key campground; 5-mile loop from the trailhead to Gate 2, then west on Research Road to Gate 2B, and then north to the Long Pine Key campground.

DIFFICULTY: Easy to moderate.

TIME REQUIRED: 2 to 4 hours.

SPECIAL CONCERNS: Mosquitoes and biting flies in summer and fall. Sharp, jagged limestone (pinnacle rock) is exposed in pine rocklands, so off-trail travelers should wear appropriate shoes such as hiking boots, sneakers, or other rugged footwear.

SCENIC VALUE: Excellent. Many first-time visitors may find pine rock-

Gate 3 Firebreak Trail

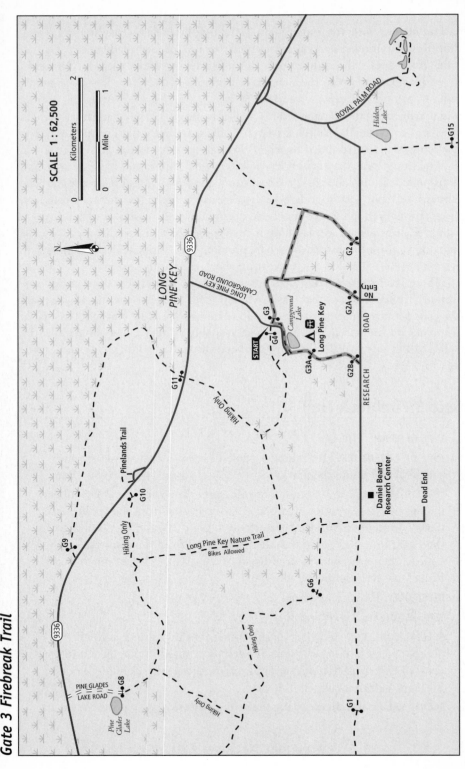

SCALE 1 : 62,500

Kilometers
0   1   2

Mile
0   1

N

LONG PINE KEY

9336

LONG PINE KEY CAMPGROUND ROAD

ROYAL PALM ROAD

Hidden Lake

G15

G2

No Entry

G2A

RESEARCH ROAD

G3

Campground Lake

Long Pine Key

G4

START

G3A

G2B

Hiking Only

G11

Pinelands Trail

G10

Long Pine Key Nature Trail
Bikes Allowed

G9

Hiking Only

Daniel Beard Research Center

Dead End

G6

Hiking Only

G1

Hiking Only

PINE GLADES LAKE ROAD

G8

Pine Glades Lake

9336

land habitat monotonous, but this is one of the most floristically diverse habitats in Florida. The prairies may look homogenous too, unless you take the time to walk out into them and do some off-trail exploring.

OVERVIEW AND TRAIL DESCRIPTION: The trailhead (Gate 3) is 1.25 miles from the main park road on the left side of the Long Pine Key campground road. It is marked by signs indicating that it is available for hikers but not cyclists. The firebreaks (old logging roads) that crisscross Long Pine Key offer easy and scenic getaways for visitors seeking quiet solitude off the beaten path. This hiking trail terminates at a paved road that leads west to the Daniel Beard Research Center, or east to the main road to Royal Palm Hammock. The trail begins at a small hardwood hammock named Redd Hammock. There are no official trails into this hammock, but there are some access points along the edge; however,

Exposed limestone in rocky prairies and pine rocklands of Long Pine Key in Everglades National Park can make hiking off-trail a challenging task.

much of this hammock burned in a wildfire in 2005 and may not be accessible. The edges of hammocks are always good places to watch for warblers, vireos, flycatchers, and other spring and fall migratory birds.

There are a number of options when hiking this trail. Most hikers simply explore for a distance and then turn around, but there are some loop trails if you want a longer excursion. Refer to the map for these options, but note that a part of the loop will include walking along the swale of Research Road. This, however, can sometimes be an interesting area to see white-tailed deer and other animals along the roadside. During the cool winter months it is not uncommon to see snakes warming themselves on the asphalt. These may include large Eastern diamondback rattlesnakes, so always expect the unexpected.

A female white-tailed deer stands in a saw-grass prairie along the main park road in Everglades National Park.

Long Pine Key Nature Trail (Gate 4 to Gate 8)

TYPE OF TRAIL: Hiking or biking (National Park Service rangers and researchers occasionally drive vehicles along this trail).

TYPE OF ADVENTURE: Bike or hike along a graded firebreak that traverses pine rockland and prairie habitats, with options to explore nearby hammocks.

TOTAL DISTANCE: 12 miles round-trip (but read the notes at the end of this trail description).

DIFFICULTY: Easy to moderate.

TIME REQUIRED: A half to a full day.

SPECIAL CONCERNS: Mosquitoes and biting flies in summer and fall. Bring water and snacks if you plan on traveling the entire trail. Mountain (or hybrid) bikes are advised because rough, rocky areas occur whenever the trail crosses open prairie habitat. These same areas may be flooded during the rainy season with water up to 12 inches deep across the trail.

SCENIC VALUE: Excellent. The trail traverses pristine upland and wetland habitats.

Long Pine Key Nature Trail (Gate 4 to Gate 8)

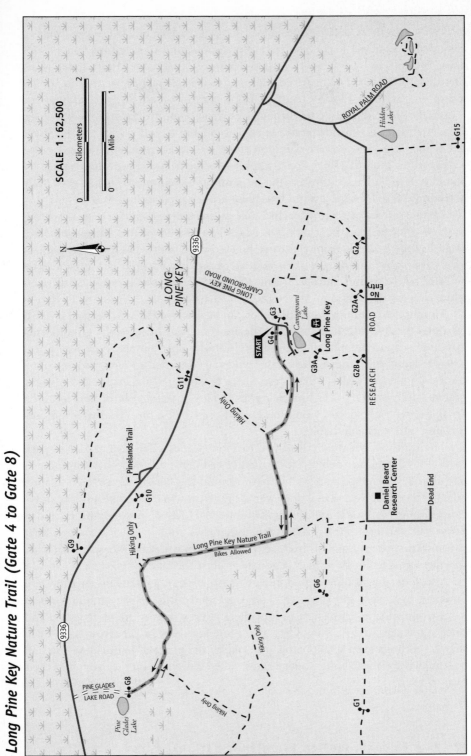

OVERVIEW AND TRAIL DESCRIPTION: This is one of the best and little-used trails in Everglades National Park. The trail offers opportunities to explore pine rockland, prairie, and tropical hardwood hammock habitats. White-tailed deer often can be seen on or near the trail, and this is also where a truly fortunate visitor might see a Florida panther. Look for animal tracks in muddy areas, especially where the trail cuts through prairie habitat. Tracks may include deer, raccoons, bobcats, Florida panthers, snakes, alligators, and wading birds. Small oak toads *(Bufo quercicus)* are common along the trail as well, and these are typically only ½ inch to 1 inch long. Explore the open prairies on foot to see an abundance of native wildflowers but be cautious of venomous snakes, especially cottonmouth moccasins around low-lying areas with standing water.

The terrestrial grass-pink orchid *(Calopogon tuberosus)* can be seen flowering in these prairies from February into May. The flowers of this attractive native orchid range in color from rich rosy pink to pure white and are produced on stems that stand above the surrounding grasses. It is often accompanied by another native orchid, the spring ladies' tresses *(Spiranthes vernalis)*, with small white flowers that spiral up the stem.

Among the common butterflies that can be observed along this trail are two rarities—the Florida leafwing and Bartram's scrub-hairstreak. The Florida leafwing is a fast-flying reddish-orange butterfly that closely resembles a leaf when it lands (the undersides of the wings are mottled grayish brown). Bartram's scrub-hairstreak is bluish gray with a few bold, white stripes and a bright orange patch on the lower hind wing. If you are interested in butterflies, look for these two rare species along the Long Pine Key Nature Trail where it cuts through pine rockland habitat.

The trail will eventually lead you to Pine Glades Lake near the main park road. This is a good rest stop for a picnic. Fishing is allowed but swimming is prohibited. There is a narrow footpath around the lake that's a nice half-mile hike for those interested in wildflowers. This path was created by anglers and is worn enough to be easily visible (always be alert for alligators lying in trails). From fall through spring there are sometimes thousands of swallows that swarm across the surface of this lake to get a sip of water on the wing. This is a spectacular sight if you're lucky enough to be at the lake for this event.

Also look for swallow-tailed kites soaring above the lake and surrounding pineland in spring and summer. These graceful birds of prey migrate north from tropical America to nest in Florida, and they're very adept at seeing and catching snakes and lizards. They also hunt for nests of other birds and will snatch nestlings even while being attacked by the parents. Witnessing this can be somewhat disheartening, but swallow-tailed kites have hungry young of their own to feed.

Although this can be a loop trail by returning to the Long Pine Key turnoff via the main park road, it is safer to return the same way you came.

Note: Be sure you stay on the same trail that you took to get to Pine Glades Lake. There are other turnoffs that can take you many miles into Long Pine Key (and are off limits to bicycles). The free map, Hiking and Biking Trails of Long Pine Key, is good to have with you or, if you are a high-tech traveler, a handheld GPS will also keep you from getting impossibly lost. The National Geographic Trails Illustrated Chart #243 (Everglades National Park) is also very useful for these trails (this chart is available at visitor center bookstores in Everglades National Park). The Long Pine Key Nature Trail (Gate 4 to Gate 8) is the only sanctioned bicycling trail on Long Pine Key. All others are for hiking only.

Another Note: A much shorter loop trail (hiking only) is available from Gate 4 by following the narrow but well-defined foot path to the left after you have reached the far side of the first Everglades prairie. This path forks once you have crossed the prairie. Taking the right fork will lead you directly through Mosier Hammock. Taking the left fork will lead you around the hammock. Both options will terminate at the Long Pine Key campground lake. Once you reach the lake, bear to the left and you will arrive at the Long Pine Key road that leads back to the trailhead. Restrooms and water are available next to the picnic area on your way back.

Mosier Hammock Trail

TYPE OF TRAIL: Hiking.

TYPE OF ADVENTURE: Hike through a pristine tropical hardwood forest.

TOTAL DISTANCE: 0.25 mile.

DIFFICULTY: Easy.

TIME REQUIRED: Half an hour.

SPECIAL CONCERNS: Exposed tree roots and limestone on the trail. Mosquitoes and biting flies in summer and fall.

SCENIC VALUE: Good. This is a scenic inside view of a typical tropical hardwood forest.

OVERVIEW AND TRAIL DESCRIPTION: This can either be a short loop trail through and around the hammock or a longer hike along the narrow footpath across the open prairie to the Gate 4 firebreak trail. This hammock was named to honor the first warden of Royal Palm State Park, Charles A. Mosier (1871–1936). Royal Palm State Park was dedicated in 1916 but was incorporated into Everglades National Park in 1947. Look for colorful liguus (pronounced *LIG-you-us*) tree snails *(Liguus fasciatus)* on the trunks of trees along this trail. There are sixty named color forms of liguus tree snails in southern Florida, and others occur in Cuba. The name *liguus* means "banded," and these snails were what inspired the colorful patterns on clothing made by Seminole and Miccosukee Indians. Liguus tree snails are now protected by state statute from collectors. Mosier Hammock is also a good place to look for birds, especially during spring and fall migration.

Pinelands Trail

The Pinelands Trail is 2 miles west of the Long Pine Key turnoff on the main park road (SR 9336). This is a short, paved loop that traverses pine rockland habitat. If you have already hiked or biked the Long Pine Key Nature Trail, you may wish to bypass the Pinelands Trail because it will be somewhat repetitious. There are, however, a few wildflowers and other native plants that can be seen along this trail that you may have missed on other trails. If you have plenty of time, or if you haven't already hiked the firebreak trails, this trail can be rewarding, both in the number of birds and butterflies, and in the number of flowering plants you'll encounter. There are interpretive signs along the way as well as a kiosk at the trailhead. Portable restrooms are sometimes available in the parking area.

TYPE OF TRAIL: Hiking. Wheelchair accessible.

TYPE OF ADVENTURE: Walk on a short loop trail through pine rockland habitat.

TOTAL DISTANCE: 0.5 mile.

DIFFICULTY: Easy.

TIME REQUIRED: Half an hour.

SPECIAL CONCERNS: Mosquitoes and biting flies in summer and fall.

SCENIC VALUE: Good. Wildflowers can be abundant along this trail.

OVERVIEW AND TRAIL DESCRIPTION: Although this is a short paved trail, it offers a good opportunity to see and photograph many interesting and rare flowering plants. It is one of the few places in Everglades National Park where you can find Cuban Nakedwood *(Colubrina cubensis* var. *floridana)*. This rare, endangered shrub or small tree has oblong leaves that are softly hairy. The small star-shaped fragrant flowers are greenish yellow and produced in clusters. The name *nakedwood* refers to the shedding bark. An endemic morning-glory relative, pineland clustervine *(Jacquemontia curtisii)*, is rather abundant along this trail. It is a petite vine with half-inch starlike white flowers that glisten in the sunlight.

Look for it climbing around on shrubs along the trail. In the cool winter months, also look for snakes lying on the warm asphalt of this trail. Remember, only lucky visitors get to see snakes in the Everglades!

There are also three attractive day-flying moths that can be seen in this region. The bella moth is small, but it flashes pink on the wings when in flight. The faithful beauty is boldly and patriotically colored red, white, and blue. The wings are blue with white spots, and there is a patch of red on the hind wing. Another colorful moth is the polka-dot wasp-moth, or oleander moth. It has the shape of a wasp but with an orange abdomen and dark blue wings dotted with white spots. The larvae of the latter two species feed on members of the poisonous dogbane family (Apocynaceae), so their bright colors serve as a warning to would-be predators.

Pine Glades Lake and Gate 8 Loop Trail (Long Pine Key Nature Trail West Entrance)

Pine Glades Lake is accessible by vehicle off of the main park road (SR 9336) by taking the second left turnoff, heading west after the Pinelands Trail. The first left is a gated firebreak (Gate 10) that leads to the Long Pine Key Nature Trail as well. The Pine Glades Lake turnoff is not indicated by signs and is therefore often missed by visitors. This is a dirt road that may be partly flooded during the wet season, but the open parking area next to the lake will be dry.

TYPE OF TRAIL: Hiking or biking.

TYPE OF ADVENTURE: Varies. This can simply be a stop to enjoy the scenery and to look for birds and wildflowers around the lake, or a starting point for a much longer hiking or biking trip. The Long Pine Key Nature Trail terminates at Pine Glades Lake, but there's certainly nothing wrong with hiking or biking it from Gate 8 instead.

TOTAL DISTANCE: Varies. The footpath around Pine Glades Lake is about half a mile; a 9-mile loop trail for hiking is available from Gate 8; from Gate 8 bikers and hikers can enjoy a 12-mile round-trip excursion to Gate 4. Hikers may also explore the firebreak trails off the Long Pine Key Nature Trail. Note: These side trails are closed to bikers.

DIFFICULTY: Easy to moderate.

TIME REQUIRED: Varies. A hike around Pine Glades Lake will take about 20 to 30 minutes; hiking the 9-mile loop trail should take about 3 to 4 hours; biking the 12-mile Long Pine Key Nature Trail takes about half a day.

SPECIAL CONCERNS: Mosquitoes and biting flies in summer and fall.

Pine Glades Lake and Gate 8 Loop Trail (Long Pine Key Nature Trail West Entrance)

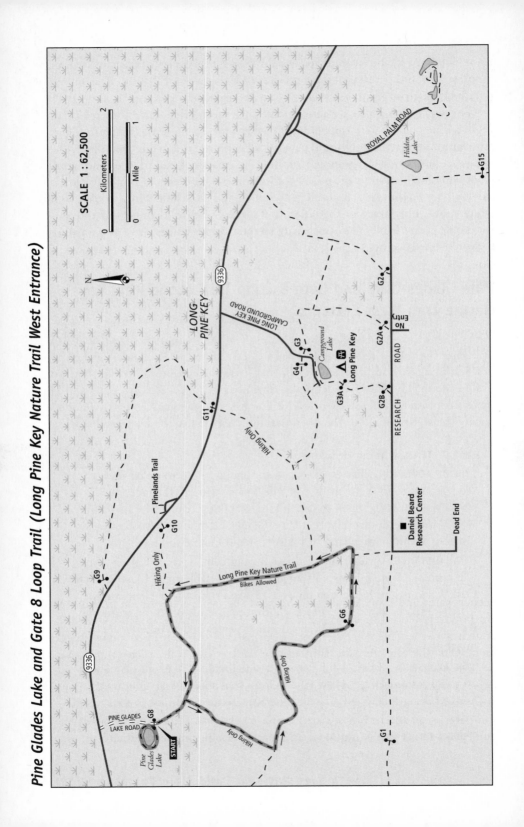

Watch for alligators or possibly cottonmouth moccasins lying next to, or on, the footpath around Pine Glades Lake.

SCENIC VALUE: Excellent. There are scenic vistas of prairie and pine rockland habitats across the lake.

OVERVIEW AND TRAIL DESCRIPTION: Pine Glades Lake was dredged for fill to build the main park road that leads to Flamingo. Fishing is allowed but swimming is prohibited. Because this lake is infrequently visited, it can be a nice quiet place to picnic or to just sit and enjoy the scenery and solitude. This can also be a rewarding spot for birders as well. A number of native wildflowers can be found around the lake and in the adjacent habitats. The firebreak past Gate 8 offers miles of exploring opportunities if you bypassed the eastern entrance at Gate 4 along the Long Pine Key turnoff. The hiking or biking distance from Gate 8 to Gate 4 and back is 12 miles.

A 9-mile loop for hiking only is available by hiking from Gate 8 south to the first turn to the right. Take this trail for a little more than a mile to another intersection and turn left. This section of the trail will head east, then south, and then back east again. Proceed past Gate 6 for about a mile until the trail takes a hard left (do not take the trail to the right just before this turn). Continue north for a little more than 2 miles to a bend to the left and follow this back to the trailhead at Gate 8. The right turn at that bend leads to Gate 10 at the main park road, so be sure you stay on the Long Pine Key Nature Trail.

Rock Reef Pass and Dwarf Cypress Forest

Tourists from mountainous regions always get a laugh when they see the signs that read ROCK REEF PASS–ELEVATION 3 FEET and DWARF CYPRESS FOREST—ELEVATION 4 FEET. There are no trails at Rock Reef Pass except for a short, elevated boardwalk with interpretive signage. This area is characterized by open prairie with scattered cypress trees, most of which are stunted because of shallow soils with few available nutrients. Occasionally, however, these are interrupted by stands of taller cypress called cypress domes, which occur in areas of deeper water and more fertile soil. Most of the cypress trees seen in this area are pond-cypress (*Taxodium ascendens*), a species characterized by ascending branches and leaflets that are mostly appressed to the stem. Most tourists see them when the branches are bare because the trees drop their leaves in winter.

Traveling west about a mile past the Pa-Hay-Okee sign, you will come to a large cypress dome that borders the south side of the main park road. If you don't mind getting your feet wet—maybe even up to your waist in the wet season—this is an interesting cypress dome to explore. Park rangers often lead guided "swamp walks" into this dome as well. There is a deep alligator hole in

The Dwarf Cypress Forest sign along the main park road in Everglades National Park is a reminder that the Everglades are not only flat, but also low-lying.

the center, so be a bit cautious if the resident alligator is present. Also watch for cottonmouth moccasins, one of four venomous snakes in the Everglades. But if you are the adventurous type, this dome has some fascinating epiphytic plants growing on the cypress trees and there are almost always barred owls present here. They are inquisitive and may fly to nearby trees to get a better look at who has intruded into their territory. This, in turn, will give you a good look at the owls. The interior of domes such as this will make you forget, if only for a brief moment, that there is a paved road just a short distance away. If you walk through the dome and come out on the south side, you will have a spectacular bird's-eye view of a vast Everglades prairie studded with dwarf cypress trees.

The name *Pa-Hay-Okee* comes from the language of the Seminole Indians and translates to "grassy waters." Bring your camera because this elevated overlook gives you the opportunity to see, and better appreciate, the vastness of the region that famed author Marjory Stoneman Douglas called a "River of Grass."

TYPE OF TRAIL: Elevated wood boardwalk leading to a sheltered overlook. Wheelchair accessible.

TYPE OF ADVENTURE: Walking.

TOTAL DISTANCE: 0.25 mile.

DIFFICULTY: Easy.

TIME REQUIRED: 15 to 30 minutes, depending on how long you want to enjoy the scenery.

SPECIAL CONCERNS: None. There are stairs leading up the east (right) side of the overlook, and a wheelchair accessible ramp is on the west (left) side. Mosquitoes are generally at tolerable levels even in summer.

SCENIC VALUE: Exceptional. This is one of the best scenic vistas and photo opportunities in Everglades National Park.

OVERVIEW AND TRAIL DESCRIPTION: The view to the north from the overlook encompasses the southern edge of the Shark River Slough, a broad expanse of saw-grass prairie dotted with tree islands through which a vast sheet of water flows southwest from the Big Cypress Swamp. This water eventually makes its way to the maze of deep tidal rivers that empty into Whitewater Bay and the Gulf of Mexico. Seminole Indians once plied this shallow grassy river in dugout canoes, poling their way slowly through the saw-grass, without the aid of compasses or GPS units!

The headwaters of the Shark River Slough can be seen at Shark Valley in the northern Everglades off of Tamiami Trail (US 41). Far to the west there is a broad expanse of mangroves along Florida's coast that grows in the brackish water created by the freshwater of the Everglades mixing with the salt water of the Gulf of Mexico. This is a biologically rich area and serves as a critical nursery ground for countless fish, crustaceans, and other marine organisms. The trees themselves offer protected areas for bird rookeries. They are also prime nesting areas for ospreys and bald eagles. So the water you see at the Pa-Hay-Okee Overlook serves a vital purpose, not only as a critical component for the health of the interior Everglades, but also for the vast mangrove swamps and brackish estuaries of the coastal regions.

The Pa-Hay-Okee Overlook offers a grand view of one of the most scenic vistas in the Everglades.

It is still possible for intrepid explorers to make their way from Shark Valley through the saw-grass to Rookery Branch and on to Whitewater Bay and Flamingo, but this requires a great deal of familiarity with the region. This route is impassable during the dry season, so it must be undertaken when water levels are high in the rainy summer months. Needless to say, it can easily become a trip filled with misery, fatigue, and countless questions about one's sanity. Sleeping in a canoe or a flat-bottomed poling skiff in the middle of a sea of saw-grass in the summer is not the height of camping comfort. It is certainly not a sanctioned trip by the park, and any mishap could become an emergency situation. It is best to observe this river of grass from either the Pa-Hay-Okee Overlook or the tower at Shark Valley to the north, and just imagine the hardships one would have to endure in attempting to cross this vast region.

In late spring and summer, you will have a good chance of hearing yellow-billed cuckoos calling from the tree islands near the overlook, as well as great crested flycatchers and other nesting birds.

Mahogany Hammock

TYPE OF TRAIL: Elevated boardwalk.

TYPE OF ADVENTURE: Walking.

TOTAL DISTANCE: 0.5 mile.

DIFFICULTY: Easy.

TIME REQUIRED: One half to 1 hour.

SPECIAL CONCERNS: Mosquitoes and biting flies in summer and fall.

SCENIC VALUE: Excellent. This provides a bird's-eye view of the interior of a tropical hardwood hammock surrounded by freshwater marsh.

OVERVIEW AND TRAIL DESCRIPTION: Like its name implies, West Indies mahogany trees can be found in this hammock. Mahogany Hammock is surrounded by freshwater marsh with a deeper moat adjacent to the hammock, which is created by water flow and helps spare the hammock from lightning-caused fires that race across the surrounding prairies in the rainy season. The entire region can be bone dry in spring before the rainy wet season makes its annual debut. The national champion mahogany tree can be seen adjacent to the boardwalk, its ancient trunk and limbs showing signs of past lightning strikes and hurricanes. The spreading root systems of huge fallen trees that tower above the boardwalk attest to the strength of Hurricane Andrew. This Category 5 storm, with gusting winds that exceeded 200 miles per hour, passed directly over the Everglades on August 24, 1992. An interpretive sign and photograph of the destroyed boardwalk through Mahogany Hammock is displayed along the walkway.

Mahogany Hammock is a popular roosting site for immature southern bald eagles, which can be seen either perched in trees surrounding the hammock or soaring overhead. Immature bald eagles lack the white head and tail feathers and are mostly uniformly brown. Mature bald eagles occasionally can be seen here as well. It is also a popular place for birders to observe warblers and other migratory birds, and there are resident barred owls present year-round. Listen for their loud calls, especially at dusk, that sound as if they are asking "who cooks for you, who cooks for you all?"

A rare tropical tree, myrtle-of-the-river *(Calyptranthes zuzygium)*, can be seen along the walk, along with interesting ferns, bromeliads, and both epiphytic and terrestrial native orchids. On calm days you may detect a slight skunklike odor emitted by a native tree called white stopper *(Eugenia axillaris)*. The astringent fruits of this tree were once used to treat diarrhea, hence the name "stopper."

Keep an eye out for such wildlife as Eastern indigo snakes, yellow rat snakes, and Florida kingsnakes inside the hammock, or watch for mangrove water

The Mahogany Hammock boardwalk invites visitors to explore the interior of a shady tropical hardwood hammock.

snakes in the shallow water below the elevated boardwalk between the parking area and the hammock. There are three distinct color forms of the mangrove water snake: red, black, and straw. This is definitely a place to take your time and carefully scrutinize the surrounding forest for plants and animals that the average visitor may pass by.

Paurotis Pond

Paurotis Pond is located along the main park road between Mahogany Hammock and Nine Mile Pond. Canoeing and kayaking are allowed only during fall and winter, but it is a relatively small pond that is mainly used by anglers. It is off-limits during nesting season from spring through summer. If you are a bird-watcher visiting during the spring and summer months, this may be a worthwhile stop to view (from the shoreline) wading birds nesting and roosting in the trees surrounding this scenic pond. A spotting scope will help.

A black vulture rests atop the sign that warns canoeists and kayakers that Paurotis Pond is closed during bird-nesting season from spring through summer.

Nine Mile Pond

TYPE OF TRAIL: Canoeing or kayaking (motors prohibited).

TYPE OF ADVENTURE: Canoe or kayak along a marked trail through Everglades marsh.

TOTAL DISTANCE: 5.5 miles to complete the entire loop.

NAUTICAL CHARTS: National Geographic Trails Illustrated Chart #243 (Everglades National Park) has good detail of this trail in an inset.

DIFFICULTY: Easy to moderate.

TIME REQUIRED: 3 to 4 hours.

SPECIAL CONCERNS: Mosquitoes and biting flies in summer and fall. Impassable during times of prolonged drought.

SCENIC VALUE: Excellent.

Nine Mile Pond

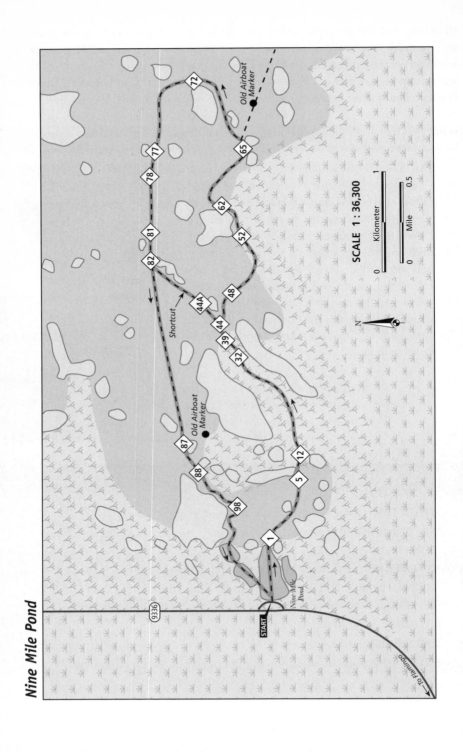

SCALE 1 : 36,300

Kilometer

Mile

OVERVIEW AND TRAIL DESCRIPTION: The trailhead is located at Nine Mile Pond and marked by signage on the south side of the main park road. When water levels are low, much of the trail is impassable, and this usually occurs during the spring dry season from March to June. This scenic canoe or kayak trail winds through shallow freshwater marsh that is studded with small tree islands, cat-tails, and red mangrove trees. Watch for alligators, a wide variety of birds, and other resident and migratory wildlife. The endangered snail kite can sometimes be seen here, along with wood storks, white pelicans, roseate spoonbills, herons, egrets, ducks, and other interesting birds. The harmless mangrove water snake can be found here, and there are three color forms of this snake in the Ever-glades region—black, straw, and red. This is also an area where visitors can see paurotis palms *(Acoelorrhaphe wrightii)* growing in their natural habitat. This state-listed endangered species occurs only in Collier, Miami-Dade, and Mon-roe Counties in Florida, and it is so attractive that it is grown commercially for landscaping. Nine Mile Pond is an easy trip for novice canoeists because it is a

Egrets and herons are common sights in the open prairies when water levels are high or receding.

shallow loop trail marked with numbered posts, and the trail is relatively protected from wind. Canoes are available here to rent during the busy tourist season (winter through spring), and park rangers also offer guided canoe trips at this location (additional fee). There is a rather steep drop-off along parts of the shoreline where you launch, so test the depth with your paddle.

Once you have launched in Nine Mile Pond, paddle due east to Marker 1, where the creek cuts through a marl prairie. Follow the marked trail to Marker 44, where you will have a decision to make: You can either take a shortcut at this junction or complete the entire loop. To take the shortcut, turn northeast to Marker 44A and on to Marker 82 on the north side of the loop, and then turn left at Marker 82 to return to Nine Mile Pond. To complete the full loop, turn southeast at Marker 44 and continue your journey.

Noble Hammock Canoe Trail

TYPE OF TRAIL: Canoe or kayak (motors prohibited).

TYPE OF ADVENTURE: Canoeing or kayaking along a loop trail through mangroves and a tropical hardwood hammock.

TOTAL DISTANCE: 2-mile loop.

DIFFICULTY: Easy.

TIME REQUIRED: 1 to 2 hours.

SPECIAL CONCERNS: Mosquitoes and biting flies in summer and fall. Some tight turns may be difficult in long kayaks.

SCENIC VALUE: Good. This trail meanders through red mangroves and passes a hardwood hammock on a shell mound where there was once an illegal moonshine operation.

OVERVIEW AND TRAIL DESCRIPTION: The Noble Hammock trailhead is marked by signage on the south side of the main park road between Nine Mile Pond and Hells Bay. This rather short canoe trail is excellent for those who either have limited time or are novice canoeists who want to sharpen their skills in a quiet protected area. There are a number of sharp turns that may be difficult for long kayaks. The trail winds through mangroves and connects to a few small ponds. Watch for mangrove cuckoos, warblers, white-crowned pigeons, and night-herons along the trail.

Noble Hammock was once the site of a bootlegger's illegal whiskey still. William "Willie" Nobles built his whiskey still along this narrow creek, and it became a popular camp. He also was the proprietor of Nobles Bakery, Meat Market and Grocery in Homestead, which opened shortly after the turn of the twentieth century. His store was sold in 1913 and then moved from its original location on the property to make room for a new bakery and grocery. Even as late as 1968, remnants of the whiskey still were present at Noble Hammock, which consisted of a wood boardwalk made of barrel staves, a brick furnace, a shallow well as a water source, and metal containers complete with deep gashes made by a law-enforcement officer's axe. Whiskey (moonshine) stills dotted the Everglades region during Prohibition (1920–1933), and some were even built in deep solution holes of hammocks to hide them from the authorities. The lawlessness of the Everglades in those days was rampant, with locals poaching wildlife, shooting plume birds for the millinery trade, making moonshine, and committing murder. The rule of the day was that if you encountered anyone in the Everglades, always state why you're there, but never ask them what they're doing out there, or you may never be seen again. When asked by government officials about their source of income, most claimed to be "farmers" because they grew sugarcane to make their moonshine.

The trailhead to the Noble Hammock Canoe Trail is about 100 yards from the exit point, so you will have a short walk to your vehicle.

Hells Bay Canoe Trail

TYPE OF TRAIL: Canoeing or kayaking (no motors between the trailhead and Lard Can).

TYPE OF ADVENTURE: Canoe or kayak through a tidal mangrove forest.

TOTAL DISTANCE: From the trailhead: 3 miles to Lard Can campsite; 3.5 miles to Pearl Bay chickee (wheelchair accessible); 5.5 miles to Hells Bay chickee.

NAUTICAL CHARTS: NOAA Chart #11433 (Whitewater Bay); National Geographic Trails Illustrated Chart #243 (Everglades National Park). Use the NOAA chart for navigating.

DIFFICULTY: Easy to moderate.

TIME REQUIRED: A half to a full day, depending on how far you decide to travel.

SPECIAL CONCERNS: Intolerable mosquitoes in summer and fall, so be prepared. Backcountry permits required for camping.

SCENIC VALUE: Good. The trail meanders through mature and stunted red mangroves interspersed by saw-grass and salt-marsh vegetation. Native orchids and bromeliads grow as epiphytes on the trees along the trail.

OVERVIEW AND TRAIL DESCRIPTION: The trailhead is located between Noble Hammock Canoe Trail and West Lake on the north side of the main park road and

Hells Bay Canoe Trail

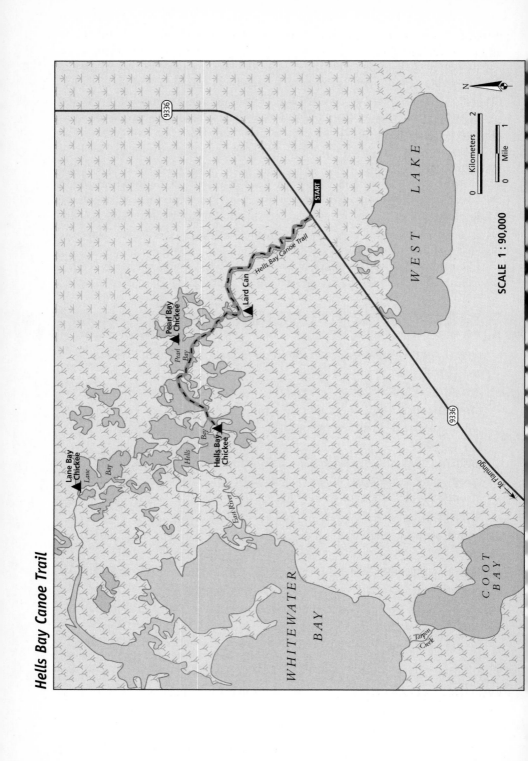

WHITEWATER BAY

COOT BAY

Tarpon Creek

WEST LAKE

9336

9336

to Flamingo

START

Lard Can

Hells Bay Canoe Trail

Pearl Bay Chickee

Pearl Bay

Hells Bay Chickee

Hells Bay

East River

Lane Bay Chickee

Lane Bay

N

0   Kilometers   2
0   Mile   1

SCALE 1 : 90,000

is marked by signage. The trailhead has a small dock for loading and unloading and is located in a sheltered dome of mangroves. Salt-marsh mosquitoes can be unbearable in summer and fall, and their numbers will remain high until finally quelled by the first cold snaps of winter, usually sometime in December. Old-timers used to complain that Hells Bay was "hell to get into and hell to get out of," but that's not so true today with the marked trail and campsites now available to canoeists and kayakers.

If you plan on camping, Lard Can is a land-based campsite and Pearl Bay and Hells Bay are both elevated wood chickees. There are some tight turns along this trail, so long kayaks may have difficulty maneuvering in some places. Otherwise, it is a nice protected trail that is a good choice when winds are strong. Fishing can be excellent as well, and fish to target in this area are mangrove snapper, snook, and redfish. Be sure to check park regulations regarding seasons, size limits, possession limits, and fishing-license requirements if you plan on fishing. Also be aware that powerboats can access this area from White-water Bay, but motors are prohibited from the trailhead to the Lard Can campsite. Lard Can is limited to ten campers, Pearl Bay chickee (wheelchair accessible) is limited to six campers on each side of the chickee, and the same is true for Hells Bay chickee. Whitewater Bay can be accessed from the Hells Bay chickee by following the East River westward, and this could be a planned loop back to Flamingo. Once you reach Whitewater Bay, Flamingo is a 6.5-mile paddle. You must, of course, have a vehicle at Flamingo if you need to return to the Hells Bay Canoe Trail trailhead.

If you decide to explore off the marked trail in a canoe or kayak in the Hells Bay region, be absolutely certain that you do so with extreme caution. This is an area where you can become impossibly lost in very short order (look at your chart and you'll see why). The Hells Bay area is a complex and confusing maze of mangrove islands, creeks, lakes, and ponds that all start to look alike after a while. It is highly advisable to stay on the trail if you are unfamiliar with the Everglades backcountry and especially if you are not in possession of a GPS unit (with spare batteries!).

Although mangrove habitat is relatively repetitious, the wormvine orchid (*Vanilla barbellata*), dollar orchid (*Prosthechea boothiana*), butterfly orchid (*Encyclia tampensis*), and interesting bromeliads such as the powdery catopsis (*Catopsis berteroniana*) can be seen along the Hells Bay Canoe Trail. Unfortunately for most explorers of this trail, all of these species flower in summer or early fall. The wormvine orchid flowers are especially attractive and have a delightful scent, but the flowers appear in May and June. Admiring their beauty and heavenly aroma will require tolerating the horror of thousands of salt-marsh mosquitoes attempting to make you a part of a food chain! But once you see the flowers, all else will seem eclipsed, if only for a very brief moment until the real-

The attractive flowers of the native wormvine orchid (Vanilla barbellata) *appear right when thick swarms of salt-marsh mosquitoes make their spring debut.*

ity of summer in the mangroves returns. Look also for the mangrove rubber vine *(Rhabdadenia biflora)*, which has usually paired white trumpet-shaped flowers and a yellow throat.

Note: There are four other chickees in remote areas east of Whitewater Bay and north of Hells Bay. Three of them can be reached via an inside route through the maze of mangrove islands from the Hells Bay chickee. These are the Lane Bay chickee, Roberts River chickee, and North River chickee. The fourth is the Watson chickee near the Watson River in the northeast corner of Whitewater Bay. All four of them can also be reached from Flamingo by taking Buttonwood Canal to Coot Bay and then through Tarpon Creek to Whitewater Bay. Whitewater Bay can be very rough in windy conditions, so canoeists should be especially careful. And it is very easy to get lost in this region—pay very close attention to your nautical chart.

About Getting Lost

If you think you are lost in the Hells Bay region, don't panic! Assess your surroundings, check your compass (you did remember to bring one, didn't you?), and consult your chart (use the NOAA Nautical Chart #11433 [Whitewater Bay] for navigation). If you don't have a chart with you, think about how dumb you feel! Try to retrace your path soon after you got the feeling that you are lost, but don't go too far if you are not sure about which direction you need to be heading or you may make the situation even worse. When you left the marked trail, was the tide flowing with you or against you? If it was with you (outgoing) then you need to paddle against it to return to the trail. Needless to say, a GPS unit can save you from all of this grief and worry, so if you don't have one when you get lost the first time, my personal advice is to purchase one and learn how to use it before you get lost again.

If you decide that you are impossibly lost and it's not an emergency situation, the smart thing to do is to take whatever openings in the maze of mangroves that lead west (toward sunset). Once you are in Whitewater Bay, follow the southern shoreline to Tarpon Creek (Marker 10), and this will lead you south into Coot Bay. If you are in a canoe and Coot Bay is choppy, stay close to the shoreline until you come to the entrance to Buttonwood Canal (Marker 2). This will lead you back to Flamingo, and civilization.

If you are in a life-threatening situation or have a medical emergency, see Emergency Situations in Appendix B.

West Lake–Alligator Creek Canoe Trail

TYPE OF TRAIL: Canoeing or kayaking (vessels with outboard motors of six-horsepower or less are allowed in West Lake, but no farther).

TYPE OF ADVENTURE: Canoe or kayak across open bays and through mangrove-lined creeks and ponds.

TOTAL DISTANCE: 8.5 miles from the ramp at West Lake to the Alligator Creek campsite.

NAUTICAL CHARTS: NOAA Chart #11433 (Whitewater Bay); National Geographic Trails Illustrated Chart #243 (Everglades National Park).

DIFFICULTY: Moderate to strenuous, depending on wind conditions.

TIME REQUIRED: 3 hours or more to reach the campsite.

SPECIAL CONCERNS: Mosquitoes and biting flies in summer and fall. Wind can create rough conditions for canoeists in West Lake.

West Lake–Alligator Creek Canoe Trail

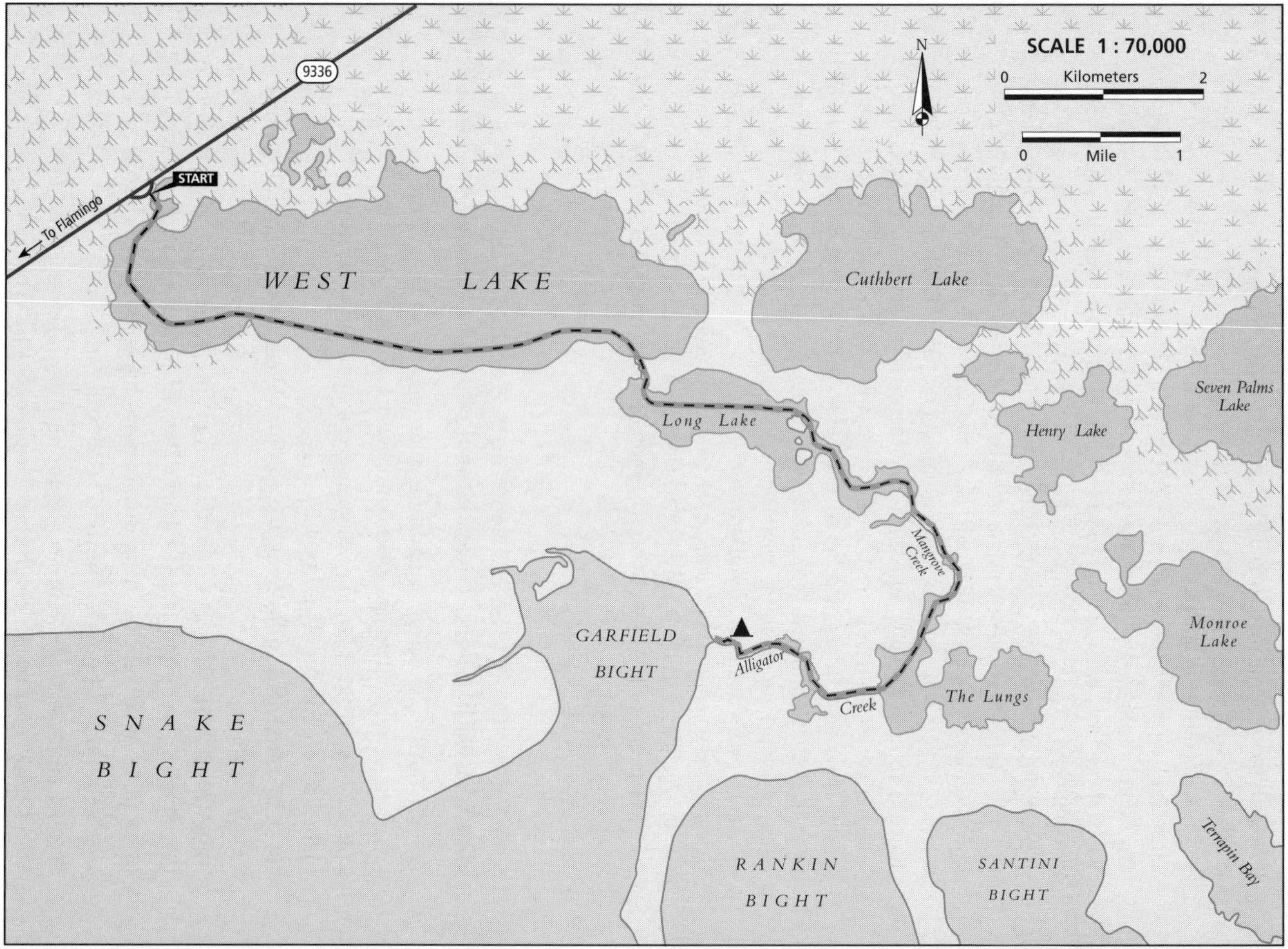

SCALE 1 : 70,000

Kilometers
0   1   2

Mile
0   1

N

to Flamingo

9336

START

WEST LAKE

Cuthbert Lake

Long Lake

Henry Lake

Seven Palms Lake

Monroe Lake

Terrapin Bay

Mangrove Creek

The Lungs

Alligator Creek

SANTINI BIGHT

RANKIN BIGHT

GARFIELD BIGHT

SNAKE BIGHT

Two canoeists explore the scenery along the edge of West Lake in Everglades National Park.

SCENIC VALUE: Excellent. The entire trail is lined with mangroves, and the creeks and ponds are very scenic.

OVERVIEW AND TRAIL DESCRIPTION: The entrance to the parking lot for West Lake is between Noble Hammock and Mrazek Pond along the main park road. There is a surface ramp, dock, picnic tables, and restroom facilities available. There is also a short walking trail accessible from the parking lot (west side) that leads into mangrove habitat to an elevated wood dock overlooking West Lake.

When launching at the West Lake boat ramp, watch for large alligators and even American crocodiles (American alligators are much more dangerous to people and pets in Florida than American crocodiles). This is an excellent trail for either a day trip or to camp up to two nights (mid-November through late April) in a remote area along the aptly named Alligator Creek. Fishing can be excellent, especially in West Lake and Long Lake, and the fish to target are spotted seatrout, snook, redfish, black drum, and mangrove snapper. Large schools of mullet can often be seen too, but these are vegetarians and will not take bait. You can see them jumping or sometimes scattering in large schools when being attacked by predatory fish such as snook, tarpon, and jacks. They are a favorite food of crocodiles, alligators, bottlenose dolphins, ospreys, bald eagles, and pelicans as well.

If winds are strong and you are in a canoe, stay close to the lee side of West Lake until you reach the protection of the creek that leads to Long Lake. If you are planning to travel the entire way to the Alligator Creek campsite, once you enter Long Lake paddle southeast to the far side of the lake to Mangrove Creek, a narrow passage that leads to another lake called The Lungs (this lake has the shape of lungs when viewed from the air, or on your chart). Stay close to the west shoreline of The Lungs until you reach Alligator Creek. Paddle west through the creek until you enter another small lake and then paddle north until the shoreline forms a narrower passage. The next section of Alligator Creek leads to the campsite. This is a land-based campsite for up to three parties with a total of eight people. There are no toilet facilities.

Alligator Creek opens into Garfield Bight, and this can be a good place to see wading birds, especially during the beginning of a rising tide or the last stages of a falling tide. This bight is very shallow and may be impassable during low tide, so if the tide is falling just before dark, do not stray too far away from your campsite or you may find yourself stranded until the tide changes. Tide permitting, you can also explore Snake Bight, Rankin Bight, Santini Bight, and Florida Bay from this location. Fishing in this area can be exceptional, and the principal fish to target include spotted seatrout, snook, and redfish. Sawfish (protected species), tarpon, and sharks patrol these shallows as well. Bottlenose dolphins and West Indian manatees can sometimes be seen in the deeper passes of Florida Bay.

Snake Bight Trail

TYPE OF TRAIL: Hiking or biking.

TYPE OF ADVENTURE: Hike or bike along a straight elevated trail through mangrove and coastal strand habitat to an elevated boardwalk at the shoreline of Snake Bight.

TOTAL DISTANCE: 1.5 miles one way.

DIFFICULTY: Easy.

TIME REQUIRED: 1 hour or more.

SPECIAL CONCERNS: Intolerable mosquitoes in summer and fall, so be prepared.

Snake Bight Trail

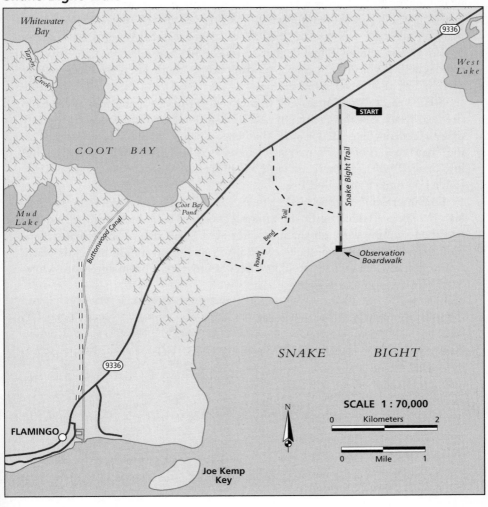

SCENIC VALUE: Good along the trail; excellent at the boardwalk overlooking Snake Bight.

OVERVIEW AND TRAIL DESCRIPTION: The trailhead is located on the south side of the main park road between West Lake and Rowdy Bend and is marked by signage. Snake Bight Trail is a favorite among birders who want to view shorebirds, egrets, herons, roseate spoonbills, white pelicans (winter–spring), brown pelicans (all year), ospreys, bald eagles, and even greater flamingos that migrate to this area in winter. Binoculars are a must and spotting scopes are also recommended. If you do not own a spotting scope, there often are birders there that do, and they never mind sharing.

Some visitors attempt to walk farther out to the shore of Snake Bight from the boardwalk, but this is not advised. The gray marl substrate has the consistency of cream cheese and is more than knee-deep in places. It is best to stay on the boardwalk. There is a narrow channel that leads from the mangroves out into Snake Bight, and there are large alligators that use this channel at high tide to feed on mullet and other fish.

One interesting wading bird that can sometimes be seen feeding in the shallows here is the reddish egret. This long-legged bird feeds by spreading its wings and then running through shallow water after small fish. The animated flapping, stretching, and spinning is comical to watch. Mature reddish egrets have a grayish body and dull red head and neck. Immature reddish egrets are white.

There are some interesting native orchids and bromeliads growing on the trees along this trail, as well as poison ivy, morning glories, coastal leather fern, and other plants that typify coastal strand and mangrove habitats. One small shrub of particular interest is the native bird pepper *(Capsicum annuum* var. *glabriusculum)*. The small ¼-inch to ⅜-inch peppers are ten times hotter than a jalapeño, but mockingbirds and catbirds gulp them whole with gusto. The peppers are red when ripe, so try one if you dare! Gulping lots of water afterwards is optional. Be sure not to wipe your eyes if you happen to get the juice on your fingers, or you'll be woefully sorry.

Poison ivy (Toxicodendron radicans) *is very common in the Everglades region. Contact with the sap can cause a blistering rash.*

There is one prominent side trail leading west off of Snake Bight Trail and this is the terminus of an extension of the Rowdy Bend Trail, which also leads back to the main park road. It too is a good hiking and biking trail. Two other less prominent trails lead east off of Snake Bight Trail, but these trails are no longer passable even though they are indicated by dotted lines on charts. The National Park Service has decided to eliminate these old trails by allowing them to become overgrown, so they advise against attempting to explore them. There is really nothing of interest along them that cannot be seen along other designated trails of the region.

Rowdy Bend Trail

TYPE OF TRAIL: Hiking or biking.

TYPE OF ADVENTURE: Hike or bike along an elevated trail that leads through mangrove, salt-marsh, and coastal strand habitats.

TOTAL DISTANCE: 2.5 miles one way.

DIFFICULTY: Easy to moderate.

TIME REQUIRED: 4 hours or more to complete the entire loop.

SPECIAL CONCERNS: Intolerable mosquitoes in summer and fall, so be prepared.

SCENIC VALUE: Good. The trail is mostly tree lined but there are some interesting native orchids, bromeliads, and other wildflowers that can be easily viewed.

OVERVIEW AND TRAIL DESCRIPTION: Rowdy Bend was once a road but is now a hiking and biking trail. The trailhead is on the south side of the main park road between Snake Bight Trail and Coot Bay Pond and is marked by signage. A fork in the trail offers two options: the left fork leads to Snake Bight Trail and the right fork loops back to the main park road. Most visitors hike or bike for a distance and then turn around and return to the trailhead. Completing the entire loop requires hiking or biking along the main park road back to the trailhead, regardless of whether you stay on Rowdy Bend Trail or divert over to Snake Bight Trail. The scenery is relatively repetitious along the entire trail, but it is interesting nonetheless.

There are possibilities to see Eastern indigo snakes, Eastern diamondback rattlesnakes, mangrove cuckoos, white-crowned pigeons, warblers, vireos, and other interesting wildlife. Look also for colorful liguus tree snails on the trunks and branches of trees along the trail.

Rowdy Bend Trail

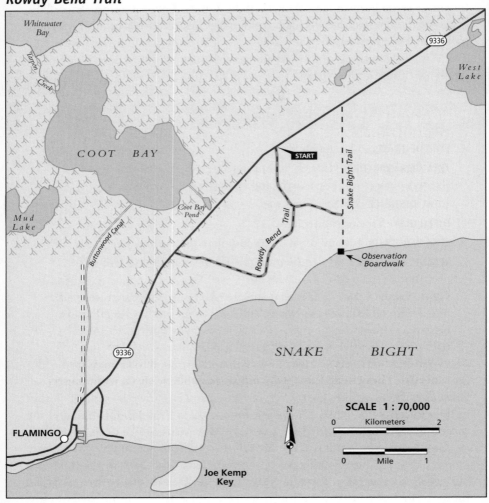

Mrazek Pond

This is not a trail, but it is a very worthwhile stopping place for birders. Sometimes this small pond is dry and practically lifeless, but other times it teems with birdlife, especially coots, gallinules, ducks, egrets, herons, roseate spoonbills, and other interesting birds of the region. Mrazek Pond is marked by signage along the main park road.

Coot Bay Pond and Mud Lake Canoe Trails

TYPE OF TRAIL: Canoeing or kayaking.

TYPE OF ADVENTURE: Canoe or kayak across open water and through mangrove-lined creeks.

TOTAL DISTANCE: 7-mile loop from Coot Bay Pond.

NAUTICAL CHARTS: NOAA Chart #11433 (Whitewater Bay); National Geographic Trails Illustrated Chart #243 (Everglades National Park).

DIFFICULTY: Moderate to strenuous, depending on wind conditions.

TIME REQUIRED: 4 hours or more, depending on weather conditions.

SPECIAL CONCERNS: Mosquitoes and biting flies in summer and fall. To complete the loop there is a portage from Homestead Canal to Buttonwood Canal. A few poisonous manchineel trees overhang the west side of Buttonwood Canal before you reach Coot Bay. (See Hazards and Health Warnings in the Introduction.) Powerboats access the backcountry by Buttonwood Canal but are required to slow down for canoeists and kayakers. Strong winds can make Coot Bay rough for canoeists. Homestead Canal may not be passable so check with rangers at Flamingo.

SCENIC VALUE: Excellent. There are scenic views of the Everglades backcountry and the opportunity for excellent bird-watching, especially in Mud Lake.

OVERVIEW AND TRAIL DESCRIPTION: This is a seldom-traveled loop trail that can be rewarding if the weather is nice. Launch at Coot Bay Pond (on the right just past Mrazek Pond). Once you cross Coot Bay Pond you will enter Coot Bay. Stay close to the southern shoreline in Coot Bay and use caution when crossing the entrance to Buttonwood Canal because of powerboat and tour boat traffic (a no-wake zone is close to the entrance, so there should not be any speeding boats in this area). Continue paddling west along the southern shoreline until you reach the entrance to a small creek on your left. This will lead you into Mud Lake, and if the tide is right, you might discover a variety of wading birds,

Coot Bay Pond and Mud Lake Canoe Trails

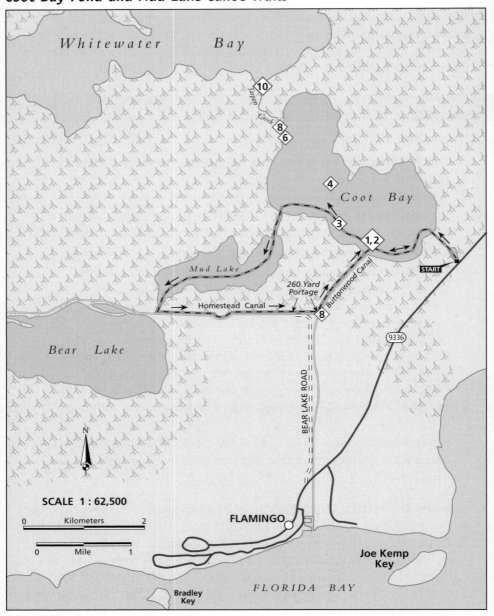

Buttonwood Canal at Flamingo offers easy access to Coot Bay, Whitewater Bay, and the vast backcountry of Everglades National Park.

including brilliant pink roseate spoonbills, feeding in the shallow water. If you enter Mud Lake at low tide close to a new moon or full moon, there may not be enough water to float a canoe (locals call this situation "where water has been"). Your only two options are to wait for the tide to change and continue on or turn around and explore Coot Bay. On the far side of Mud Lake is the entrance to Homestead Canal at Bear Lake. Turn left (east) and take Homestead Canal to its terminus. (Note: If Homestead Canal is inaccessible due to low water, you can still explore Mud Lake and return back to Coot Bay.) If Homestead Canal is accessible, you will now have to portage your canoe or kayak to a small dock along Buttonwood Canal. Proceed north in Buttonwood Canal (watch for powerboat traffic) and when you reach Coot Bay, bear to the right and follow the shoreline back to the entrance to Coot Bay Pond.

If you have the time, fishing in Coot Bay can be very good. Fish to target include spotted seatrout, snook, redfish, sheepshead, black drum, mangrove snapper, and tarpon. You can also choose to bypass the turnoff into Mud Lake and continue along the shoreline of Coot Bay to Tarpon Creek. This is a very scenic creek and popular fishing spot that leads to Whitewater Bay. Be advised that Whitewater Bay is aptly named, so paddling in open areas in a canoe when the wind strengthens can turn into a less than pleasant experience.

Christian Point Trail

There is a very narrow footpath marked by a sign on your left just before you arrive at the bridge over Buttonwood Canal at Flamingo. This trail leads to Snake Bight and is just shy of being 2 miles long one way. It winds through mangrove, salt-marsh, and coastal strand habitats. If you have explored Snake Bight Trail and/or Rowdy Bend, then this trail will be somewhat repetitious. But if you want to take a quiet stroll, it's a nice seldom-used trail and a good place to watch fishermen in boats out in Snake Bight. It's also within walking distance of the Flamingo Lodge.

Eco Pond Loop

TYPE OF TRAIL: Walking.

TYPE OF ADVENTURE: Walk along a loop trail that circles Eco Pond.

TOTAL DISTANCE: 0.5-mile loop.

DIFFICULTY: Easy.

TIME REQUIRED: 1 hour or more.

SPECIAL CONCERNS: Mosquitoes and biting flies in summer and fall. Very little shade.

About Flamingo

Many people who visit Everglades National Park get the feeling that once they reach Flamingo they have ended their Everglades adventure, and they turn around and go back. In reality Flamingo is a great jumping-off point for some of the best adventures available in the Everglades. So if you're looking for real wilderness adventure, Flamingo is a beginning, not an end. Buttonwood Canal leads north into the Everglades back-country, where you can spend a day or even weeks exploring in a canoe, kayak, or powerboat. In front of Flamingo is Florida Bay, with another wealth of exploratory options available to you. Bird-watching from a canoe or kayak can be especially rewarding in Snake Bight just east of Flamingo, especially at low tide when shorebirds and wading birds arrive to feed on crabs and other marine life stranded on the mudflats.

Flamingo was founded in 1893 when the misfits, plume hunters, gator poachers, anglers, and farmers who lived there had to choose a name for the town in order to qualify for a post office. By 1910 there were forty-five hardy people living in this remote outpost, and most called themselves "farmers" because they relied on their sugarcane crops to make illegal moonshine. The only way to get to Flamingo in those days was by boat, so it wasn't a place too often visited by law-enforcement officers, or anyone else for that matter.

There are many interesting stories about Flamingo—and some of them are even true! One of the true tales is about when Flamingo was overrun by rats, so a fellow named Gene Roberts took up a collection from the Flamingo residents and sailed off to Key West. There he offered 10 cents for each cat that was brought to the dock, which ended up costing him $40. He then took the 400 cats to Flamingo in his sailboat, claiming it was the most dreadful trip he'd ever made in his life. Once he released his boatload of cats, they reportedly scattered in every direction, but the rat population did go away after a while.

Flamingo was also a place of murder and intrigue. There is a plaque located at the base of the stairs of the Flamingo ranger station that honors Guy Bradley, a onetime resident plume hunter who was appointed as the Monroe County deputy sheriff and game warden in June 1902. He was charged with enforcing a new law that made it illegal to shoot plume birds for the millinery trade. On July 8, 1905, Bradley heard gunshots ring across Florida Bay from the Oyster Keys just offshore of Flamingo, so he made a journey out to the islands in his skiff to investigate. There he encountered Walter Smith and his two sons shooting plume birds. An argument ensued and Smith shot Bradley dead. Smith then fled to Key West, where he turned himself in, claiming self-defense. A Key West grand jury failed to indict Smith and he walked away a free man. Bradley was buried on Cape Sable, but Hurricane Donna ravaged his gravesite in 1960 and his body was lost to the sea. A park employee found his original gravestone and it is now a part of the Flamingo Visitor Center interpretive displays. A memorial plaque was donated by Tropical Audubon Society and is located outside of the Flamingo Visitor Center. It reads:

AUDUBON WARDEN WAS SHOT AND KILLED OFF THIS SHORE BY OUTLAW FEATHER HUNTERS, JULY 8, 1905. HIS MARTYRDOM CREATED NATIONWIDE INDIGNATION, STRENGTHENED BIRD PROTECTION LAWS AND HELPED BRING EVERGLADES NATIONAL PARK INTO BEING.

SCENIC VALUE: Excellent. This is one of the most popular birding locations in Everglades National Park.

OVERVIEW AND TRAIL DESCRIPTION: The turnoff to Eco Pond is just past the marina and lodge at Flamingo and is marked by signage on the right side of the main park road. The pond gets its name because it is a natural filtration system for sewerage water. It is one of the easiest places to see birds such as wood

Birds of Eco Pond

Migratory and resident birds frequent this site. Although the pond itself is man-made, the islands are natural vegetation preserved as a special roost and refuge.

Pictured here is only a small sample of birds commonly seen at Eco Pond.

Roseate Spoonbill

Eco Pond is a "must stop" for bird-watchers who visit Flamingo in Everglades National Park.

storks, roseate spoonbills, herons, egrets, bitterns, coots, ducks, gallinules, and a wide variety of other resident and migratory birds. Painted buntings are often seen here as well, and these colorful migrants are present in southern Florida from about September into May. Watch also for bald eagles, short-tailed hawks, swallow-tailed kites, and other birds of prey soaring overhead. There is an elevated wood observation platform near the trailhead and a well-worn path around the pond. If you are an avid bird-watcher, this is a good place to spend some time. Check at the Flamingo Visitor Center for reports of any unusual bird sightings around Eco Pond, or simply ask other birders along the trail. Some unusual butterflies can be observed along this trail, so it is often explored by butterfly enthusiasts as well as bird-watchers.

Alligators, fish, and a variety of turtles are always visible here, and you may even see soft-shelled turtles digging the nests where they lay dozens of white leathery eggs. The lucky ones hatch out, but many nests are discovered by marauding raccoons, as are the unattended nests of alligators. Eco Pond is another one of those spots that requires time and patience to explore. Sit for a spell and see what sort of nature event happens right before your eyes.

Flamingo to Cape Sable Route

TYPE OF TRAIL: Canoeing or kayaking (also accessible by sailboats and powerboats).

TYPE OF ADVENTURE: Canoe or kayak across mostly shallow open water (close to shore) of northern Florida Bay from Flamingo to Cape Sable.

TOTAL DISTANCE: 10 miles to East Cape; 4.5 miles from East Cape to Middle Cape; 5 miles from Middle Cape to Northwest Cape.

NAUTICAL CHARTS: NOAA Chart #11433 (Whitewater Bay); Waterproof Chart #39 (Lostmans River and Whitewater Bay); National Geographic Trails Illustrated Chart #243 (Everglades National Park); Waterproof Chart #33E (Florida Bay), including Florida Bay north to East Cape Sable.

DIFFICULTY: Moderate to strenuous.

TIME REQUIRED: Full day or more.

SPECIAL CONCERNS: Mosquitoes and biting flies in summer and fall. Strong winds create rough conditions for paddlers. There can be strong tidal flow, especially around the capes and at the entrance to East Cape Canal. Little or no shade on the beaches.

SCENIC VALUE: Excellent along the way to Cape Sable; outstanding at Cape Sable.

OVERVIEW AND TRAIL DESCRIPTION: Although this is not a designated "trail" because it crosses open water, Cape Sable is a popular destination for many people—tourists and residents alike—who want to explore and camp on one of Florida's most beautiful and pristine beaches. If you have never been to Cape Sable, you are in for a treat, weather permitting of course. Wind and tides are the two biggest obstacles to overcome, especially for canoeists. Strong south or southeast winds coupled with swift tidal flow can create very challenging conditions for any canoeist, regardless of strength and skills. The strongest winds generally occur from about midday to late afternoon, so check the weather conditions and plan your trip accordingly. Leaving early in the morning or late in the afternoon may allow you to reach Cape Sable in comparatively calm conditions. Use common sense if you plan on paddling before sunrise or after sunset—stay close to shore and have a battery-powered light in case you need to alert boaters of your location. Moreover, if winds are forecast in excess of 15 miles per hour out of the south or east and you are preparing to return to Flamingo from East Cape Sable, paddling at night may be your best option to avoid the wind and choppy conditions. Even if you leave a few hours before dawn, you will at least have a good head start before the winds pick up after sunrise.

There is, however, another option: If you are at Northwest Cape or Middle Cape, you can avoid at least some of the wind and chop by taking Middle Cape Canal (1.5 miles north of Middle Cape) into Lake Ingraham, following the marked channel southeast to East Cape Canal, and then south into Florida Bay. This will put you just east of East Cape without having to paddle in the open Gulf. Now you have a straight 9-mile paddle to Flamingo.

If you are on Cape Sable (especially Northwest Cape) and you know that choppy conditions and head winds exist in Florida Bay to the south, you can paddle north along the shoreline to Little Shark River (this is more of an option in a kayak than it is in a canoe, because it is a rather long journey and I only suggest it as a last-ditch option). But if you *do* choose this option (or you planned it in the first place), once you reach Little Shark River you can take the inside route into Oyster Bay and on to the Joe River. There is a double chickee in Oyster Bay and two more double chickees along the Joe River. By taking the Joe River back to Flamingo, you will also avoid the open water of Whitewater Bay. If you have been forced to take this route because of rough weather conditions, try to contact the Flamingo Ranger Station by cell phone or VHF marine radio to see if you can be allowed to camp at any of these campsites if you do not have a backcountry permit. Rangers take safety and weather conditions into account if your itinerary gets changed. If these chickees are full, you'll have a very long paddle back to Flamingo (or an unforgettable night sleeping in your canoe). These warnings are not intended to be intimidating; they are offered to simply inform you of your options should the weather act up. And I am speaking from personal experience!

The extraordinarily scenic beaches of Cape Sable in Everglades National Park are accessible by canoe, kayak, sailboat, or powerboat—and the sunsets are breathtaking.

Strong outgoing and incoming tides around the tip of East Cape and, especially, Middle Cape are extremely treacherous and should be avoided by canoeists. Wait for the tide to ebb or get out and portage. The same is true for Middle Cape Canal and East Cape Canal, although there are no portage options available.

Middle Cape is especially scenic, and if you have the time to make the journey, Northwest Cape is the calmest of the three capes. Cape Sable offers stunning sunsets, great fishing, and miles of pristine beach to explore. When deciding on a place to camp, first look for the long line of seaweed running parallel with the shore. This is called the wrack line, which is nothing more than sea debris left stranded at high tide. Be sure to pitch your tent landward of the wrack line or the ocean will come visit you in your tent at the next high tide. Also be advised that all campfires must be seaward of the wrack line (or at least close to it at high tide). To deter raccoons from running off with your supplies, secure your food and water before turning in for the night. Styrofoam coolers are not a deterrent for hungry raccoons, nor are conventional coolers with plastic lid latches, so either put them inside your tent with you at night or tie them closed with rope.

If you plan to fish for supper, species to target include spotted seatrout, snook, redfish, mangrove snapper, black drum, pompano, Spanish mackerel, and gafftopsail catfish. Large sharks patrol these waters very close to shore while searching for a favorite food—stingrays—so swimming is ill-advised (and there are rip currents). You will find interesting seashells washed ashore on the beach, and it is legal in Everglades National Park to collect one quart of unoccupied shells per person per day. You may also discover bits of charcoal-black pottery shards left over from now-extinct Tequesta Indians who once inhabited Cape Sable. The last of the Tequesta fled Florida to Cuba in the mid-1700s to escape war, slavery, and the genocide of diseases inadvertently introduced by Spanish explorers. Pottery shards, primitive tools made of conch shells, and the bones of the animals they ate are just about all that remain of their civilization. These historical artifacts are protected, so leave them where you found them.

Interesting plants to look for along the beachfront are sea lavender (*Argusia gnaphalodes*), bay cedar (*Suriana maritima*), sea oats (*Uniola paniculata*), and railroad vine (*Ipomoea pes-caprae*). The FalconGuide *Everglades Wildflowers* will help you identify these and other wildflowers. Enjoy your visit to Cape Sable—it is my favorite place in Florida!

Flamingo to Carl Ross Key

TYPE OF TRAIL: Canoeing or kayaking (also accessible by powerboat).

TYPE OF ADVENTURE: Canoe or kayak across northern Florida Bay and shallow flats.

TOTAL DISTANCE: 8 miles one way.

NAUTICAL CHARTS: NOAA Chart #11451 (Miami to Marathon and Florida Bay); Waterproof Chart #33E (Florida Bay).

DIFFICULTY: Moderate to strenuous depending on weather and tidal conditions.

TIME REQUIRED: A full day or more.

SPECIAL CONCERNS: Mosquitoes and biting flies in summer and fall. Rough waves and strong tides are possibilities. Because there are few trees, there is very little natural shade available. Extremely low tides around the full or new moon may make Carl Ross Key inaccessible until the tide changes.

Flamingo to Carl Ross Key

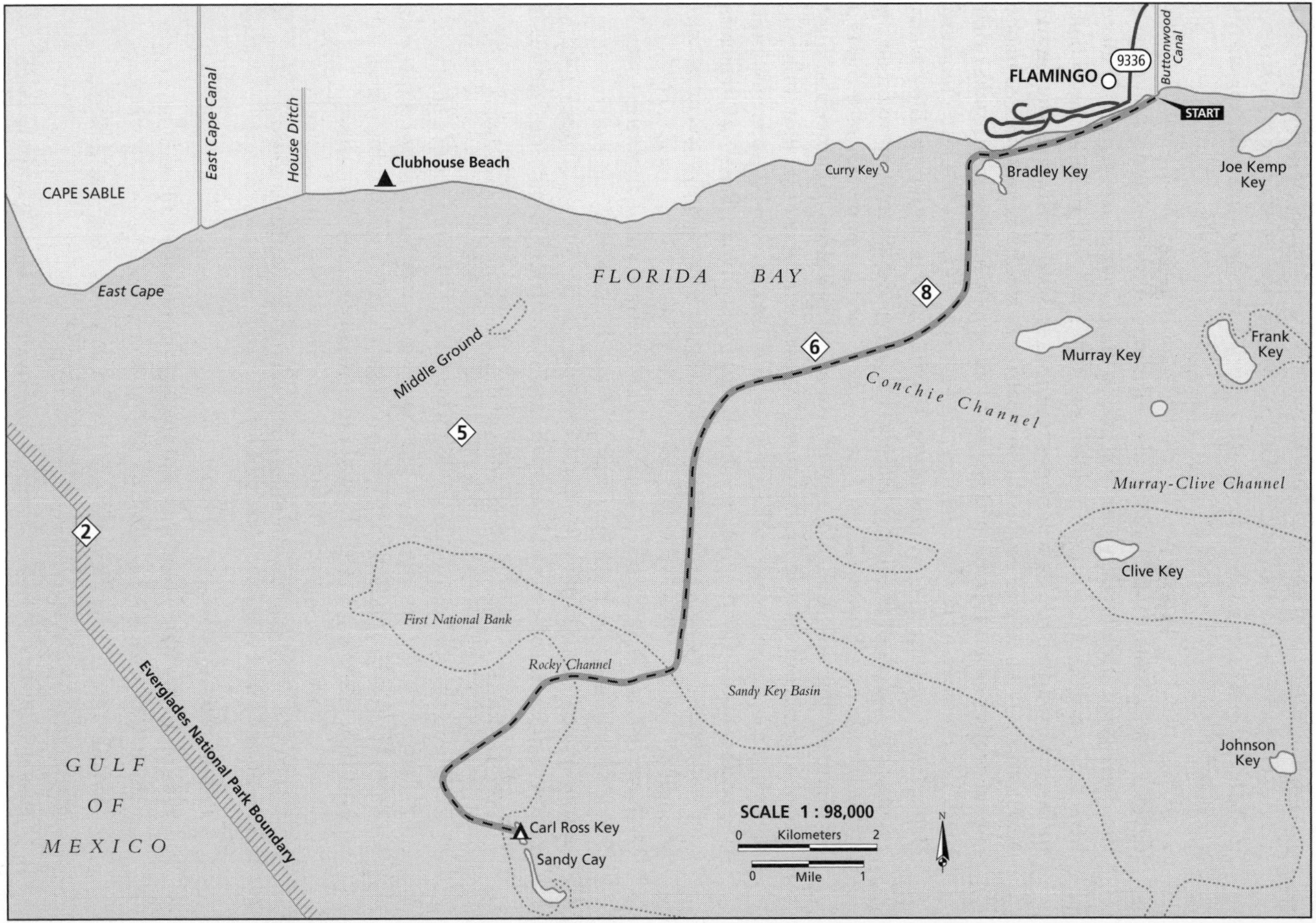

SCALE 1 : 98,000

Kilometers
0   1   2

Mile
0   1

N

FLAMINGO

9336

Buttonwood Canal

START

Joe Kemp Key

Frank Key

Murray-Clive Channel

Clive Key

Johnson Key

Murray Key

Bradley Key

Conchie Channel

8

6

Curry Key

FLORIDA BAY

Sandy Key Basin

Clubhouse Beach

5

Middle Ground

Rocky Channel

First National Bank

Carl Ross Key

Sandy Cay

House Ditch

East Cape Canal

CAPE SABLE

East Cape

Everglades National Park Boundary

2

GULF OF MEXICO

SCENIC VALUE: Excellent. This small island is remotely situated along the edge of Florida Bay and the Gulf of Mexico due south of East Cape Sable. It offers stunning sunrises over Florida Bay and romantic sunsets over the Gulf of Mexico.

OVERVIEW AND TRAIL DESCRIPTION: From Flamingo turn west and paddle along the shoreline to Bradley Key just offshore of the Flamingo campground. From here turn south-southwest and paddle toward Marker 8 in Florida Bay and on to the shallows of Dave Foy Bank that surrounds Murray Key and the Oyster Keys. It should be calmer in the shallow waters of this bank, as opposed to the deeper waters of Florida Bay. Turn west and watch for the small stakes that mark the entrance to Rocky Channel where it cuts through the First National Bank. (Don't expect an ATM machine, it's just a funny name for a shallow bank; those early settlers of Flamingo had a weird sense of humor.) Once you arrive at the entrance to Rocky Channel, it will be easier paddling unless there is a strong incoming tide. Full-moon and new-moon low tides can leave the First National Bank and even Rocky Channel exposed, so always check on tidal situations at Flamingo before embarking on your journey. If you have timed the tides right, Rocky Channel will eventually lead you to Carl Ross Key, which is an excellent and rewarding destination for campers who prefer peace, quiet, and solitude.

Next to Carl Ross Key and separated by a natural channel on the south is Sandy Cay, a major bird rookery that is closed to all entry. You can, however, paddle quietly around the island and observe a wide variety of birds such as egrets, herons, roseate spoonbills, pelicans, magnificent frigate birds, and, if you're lucky, greater flamingos. The namesakes of the historic town of Flamingo migrate to South Florida in winter and are typically seen either on Sandy Key or feeding in the shallows of Snake Bight or Garfield Bight east of Flamingo.

Fishing around Carl Ross Key and Sandy Key can be excellent, especially for seatrout, redfish, and snook. Because there are few trees on this island, it is advised that you bring a tarp or some other means of providing shade.

Coastal Prairie Trail

TYPE OF TRAIL: Hiking.

TYPE OF ADVENTURE: Hike on a trail through salt marsh and mangrove habitat along the edge of Florida Bay.

TOTAL DISTANCE: 7.5 miles one way to the Clubhouse Beach campsite.

DIFFICULTY: Moderate.

TIME REQUIRED: All day to hike the entire trail and back. Camping available.

Coastal Prairie Trail

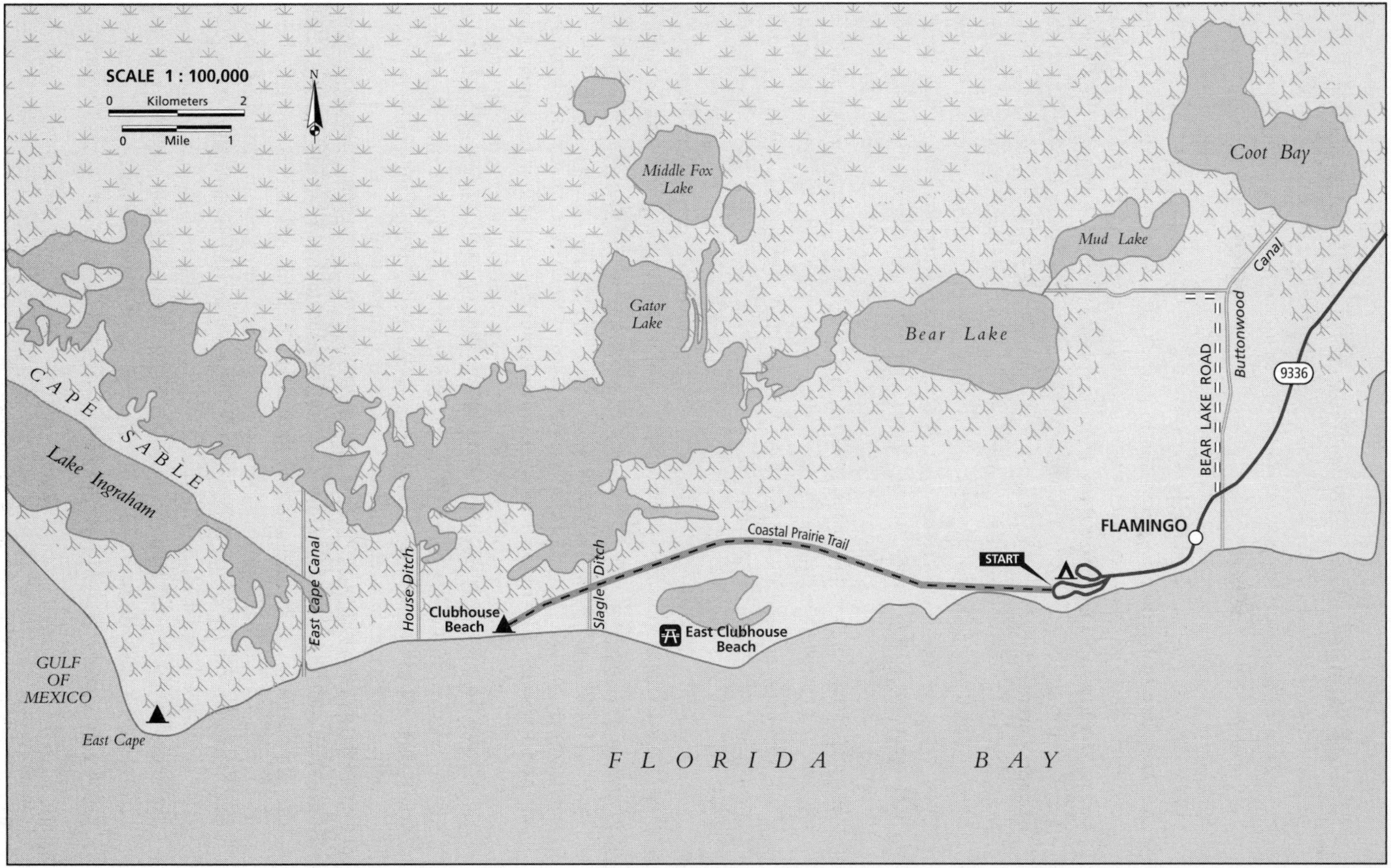

SCALE 1 : 100,000

Kilometers
0   1   2

Mile
0   1

N

Coot Bay

Canal

9336

Buttonwood Canal

BEAR LAKE ROAD

FLAMINGO

Mud Lake

Bear Lake

START

Middle Fox Lake

Gator Lake

Coastal Prairie Trail

East Clubhouse Beach

Slagle Ditch

Clubhouse Beach

House Ditch

East Cape Canal

C A P E   S A B L E

Lake Ingraham

FLORIDA   BAY

GULF OF MEXICO

East Cape

Salt-marsh prairies are found along shorelines near Flamingo in Everglades National Park.

SPECIAL CONCERNS: Mosquitoes and biting flies in summer and fall. Slippery trail when wet. Very little shade available.

SCENIC VALUE: Excellent. This trail offers a scenic view of coastal mangrove forests, extensive salt marshes, and Florida Bay.

OVERVIEW AND TRAIL DESCRIPTION: The trailhead is at the west side of Loop C in the Flamingo campground and terminates at Clubhouse Beach along the shore of Florida Bay. A backcountry permit is required to camp at East Clubhouse Beach (accessible by canoe or kayak) or Clubhouse Beach campsites. It is possible to continue west along the shoreline from Clubhouse Beach, and intrepid explorers have even hiked all the way to Cape Sable, but this requires crossing House Ditch and the more formidable East Cape Canal. The only way across East Cape Canal is to hail a boater and hitch a ride to the other side (swimming across is highly inadvisable due to boat traffic, strong tides, alligators, and large sharks). There is also a natural creek to contend with between East Cape Canal and East Cape Sable, but it is passable by wading across. Unless you are willing to endure a long and strenuous hike, it is best to access Cape Sable by canoe, kayak, sailboat, or powerboat.

The Clubhouse Beach campsites are scenic, but the waters of Florida Bay close to the shoreline are shallow and the bottom is muddy, so fishing is usually not very good at these campsites. But bird-watching can be very good, and you will see some interesting plants along the way. The salt marshes are dominated by sea blite (*Suaeda linearis*), saltwort (*Batis maritima*), sea purslane (*Sesuvium portulacastrum*), annual glasswort (*Salicornia bigelovii*), and perennial glasswort (*Sarcocornia perennis*). The leaves of these plants are edible and have a salty taste. They are high in vitamin C and have been used to ward off scurvy, a disease caused by vitamin C deficiency. If a shrub called sweetscent (*Pluchea odorata*) is flowering, you will likely be treated to an abundance of butterflies. This aster relative has tiny heads of pink flowers and is an excellent nectar source for butterflies. Look for tropical buckeyes, Florida whites, white peacocks, and other coastal butterflies that visit the flowers.

Occasionally, American crocodiles can be seen along the shoreline of Florida Bay, and always be a little bit cautious of Eastern diamondback rattlesnakes if you decide to explore off-trail in salt-marsh habitat. This large and potentially life-threatening venomous snake feeds on marsh rabbits and rodents that live in salt marshes, so it is not unusual to find one lying patiently along the small trails made by these animals. The Eastern diamondback rattlesnake is a strikingly beautiful snake, but be sure to admire it from a safe distance if you should be so lucky to come upon one in its natural habitat.

Few people hike this trail in summer but, if you do, listen for the musical, ascending buzzing calls of the prairie warbler and the sweet, high melodious notes of the Caribbean (golden) race of the yellow warbler. Both nest in the mangroves in this region, and their calls can be heard from far away. Also watch for white-crowned pigeons, mangrove cuckoos, ospreys, and bald eagles.

Everglades Wilderness Waterway

TYPE OF TRAIL: Canoeing or kayaking (or powerboat).

TYPE OF ADVENTURE: Canoe or kayak along a marked trail to backcountry campsites.

TOTAL DISTANCE: 99 miles one way.

FEE: There is a $10.00 permit fee (per group) plus a $2.00 per-person, per-day camping fee payable at either the Flamingo Visitor Center or

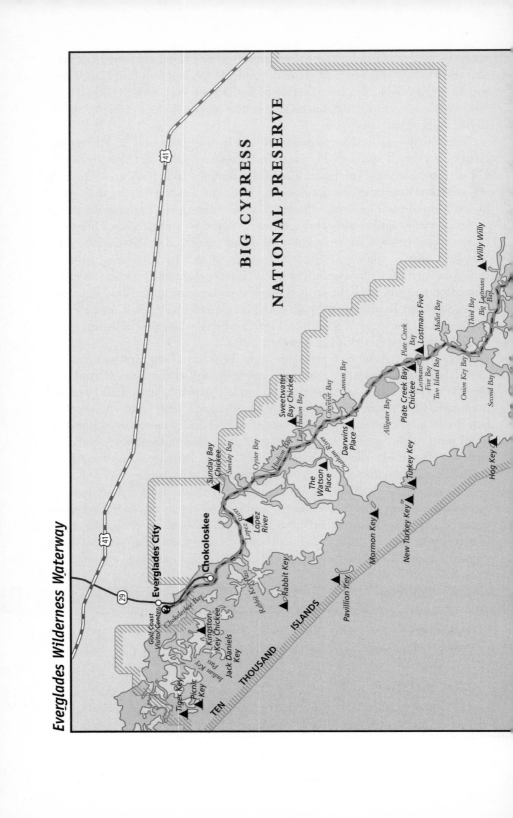

Everglades Wilderness Waterway

BIG CYPRESS

NATIONAL PRESERVE

[41]

[41]

[29] Everglades City

Chokoloskee

Gulf Coast
Visitor Center

Kingston
Key Chickee

Jack Daniels
Key

Tiger Key

Picnic
Key

Indian Key Pass

Chokoloskee Bay

TEN

THOUSAND

ISLANDS

Rabbit Key Pass

Rabbit Key

Pavillion Key

Mormon Key

New Turkey Key

Turkey Key

Hog Key

Lopez
River

Lopez River

Sunday Bay
Chickee

Sunday Bay

Oyster Bay

Hudson Bay

Last Hudson Bay

Sweetwater
Bay Chickee

The
Watson
Place

Darwins
Place

Chevelier Bay

Cannon Bay

Indian Key

Alligator Bay

Plate Creek Bay
Chickee

Lostmans
Five Bay

Plate Creek
Bay

Lostmans Five

Mullet Bay

Two Island Bay

Onion Key Bay

Second Bay

Third Bay

Big Lostmans
Bay

Willy Willy

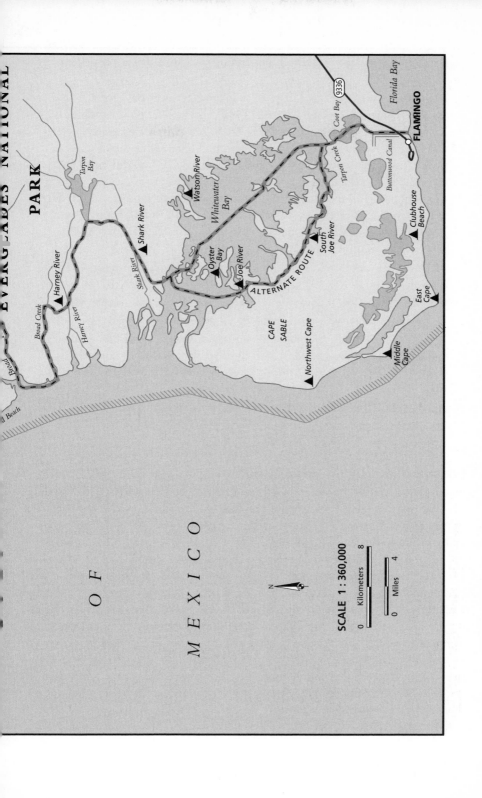

EVERGLADES NATIONAL PARK

GULF OF MEXICO

Broad Beach

Broad Creek

Broad Creek

Harney River

Harney River

Tarpon Bay

Shark River

Shark River

Watson River

Whitewater Bay

Oyster Bay

Joe River

CAPE SABLE

Northwest Cape

Middle Cape

East Cape

ALTERNATE ROUTE

South Joe River

Clubhouse Beach

Buttonwood Canal

Tarpon Creek

Coot Bay

9936

FLAMINGO

Florida Bay

SCALE 1 : 360,000

N

0   Kilometers   8

0   Miles   4

the Gulf Coast Visitor Center, depending on which direction you are paddling.

NAUTICAL CHARTS: NOAA Chart #11433 (Whitewater Bay) for the southern portion; NOAA Chart #11432 (Shark River to Lostmans River) for the central portion; NOAA Chart #11430 (Lostmans River to Wiggins Pass) for the northern section. There are also two water-proof charts that cover the same area that have GPS coordinates, but the scale is smaller than the NOAA charts. These are Everglades & Ten Thousand Islands (Chart #41) for the northern region, and Lost-mans River & Whitewater Bay (Chart #39) for the southern region. You can also use National Geographic Trails Illustrated Chart #243 (Everglades National Park).

DIFFICULTY: Moderate to strenuous depending on tide and weather conditions.

TIME REQUIRED: 7 to 9 days one way by canoe; 4 to 5 days one way by kayak; an average of 6 hours one way by powerboat.

SPECIAL CONCERNS: Intolerable mosquitoes in summer and fall, especially at night, so be prepared. Strong tidal flow and swift currents in rivers that connect to the Gulf of Mexico. Wind can be a problem in open water.

SCENIC VALUE: Excellent. Although most of the trip is through mangrove-lined creeks, rivers, and bays, this is one of the best wilderness excursions in all of Florida.

OVERVIEW AND TRAIL DESCRIPTION: This is wild Florida at its best. The trail begins at Flamingo for those heading north, or at Everglades City for those heading south. There are private services at Everglades City that will rent canoes and either pick you up when you arrive at Flamingo and transport you and your gear back to Everglades City or drive your vehicle to Flamingo while you are on the Wilderness Waterway. You can then simply pick up your keys from the dock master once you turn in your canoe. Everglades National Park backcountry camping permits are mandatory. Have your itinerary planned when you show up at the ranger station, because once your itinerary is entered into the park computer, you will know right away whether or not your chosen campsites are available for you or your group. If you are attempting the trip in December or January, you may have to adjust your itinerary to other available sites, or perhaps even schedule more than a one-night stay at a campsite until the next one is available. Distances between campsites vary, but most are less than 10 miles apart and can easily be reached in six hours or less, even in inclement weather.

A serene river leads to Lostmans Five Bay along the 99-mile Everglades Wilderness Waterway.

Do not treat this trip lightly, and definitely do not overestimate your abilities. If you are a novice canoeist, sharpen your skills elsewhere before attempting such a long and oftentimes difficult trip. Tides can be especially difficult to paddle against in a canoe, and cold fronts can bring rain and strong winds without much advance warning. Safely exploring the Everglades backcountry requires careful planning and preparation, so check with park rangers for advice if needed.

If you purchase nonwaterproof NOAA charts (the best in my opinion because of the larger scale than the waterproof charts), cut the charts into sections and have them laminated. This protects them from water damage and makes the charts easier to use. Be sure to label the top, bottom, and sides of each section so you will know which one connects to the other. Put them in a binder of some sort and you're all set.

I also recommend taking along the small spiral-bound booklet *A Guide to the Wilderness Waterway of the Everglades National Park* (available at all retail shops in Everglades National Park). It has the entire trail broken down in 2 to 3 mile sections, and, therefore, the scale is much larger than on any of the nautical charts.

There are more than thirty campsites available along the Wilderness Waterway, with more than twenty of them land-based. The others are elevated chickees, either single or double, that consist of a wood dock with a roof and portable toilet. Be advised, however, that many of the land-based campsites are along the coastline of the Gulf of Mexico in the Ten Thousand Islands region, and they are in exposed positions. Canoeists should check the weather and utilize the interior campsites and chickees to avoid paddling in open water if storms or strong winds are predicted.

Be advised too that The Nightmare is impassable at low tide, even in a canoe (you will be left stranded in mud where portaging is impossible). If you are about to enter The Nightmare and the tide is falling, you should either take the outside route from the Broad River to the Harney River along the edge of the Gulf of Mexico, weather permitting of course, or wait until the tide changes. The Nightmare is nothing more than a narrow winding creek through a dense mangrove forest, so don't think that it's somehow any spookier than other creeks along the waterway. If you do get stranded in The Nightmare at low tide, you have a couple of hours to watch fiddler crabs in the exposed mud and mangrove crabs on the trees. On occasion you may have to portage over fallen trees in The Nightmare.

In the northern half of the Wilderness Waterway, especially when crossing some of the larger interior bays, pay very close attention to the markers because they are smaller than those in the southern half of the waterway. If islands are not matching up to those on your chart, stop and hold your position until you get it figured out, even if you have to backtrack to the previous marker. It is wise to have binoculars on board for this very purpose. Another tip is to sit and watch for powerboats traversing the marked waterway and then paddle accordingly.

If you need further information, you may find answers to you questions at www.nps.gov/ever.

Everglades National Park, Shark Valley

The Shark Valley entrance to Everglades National Park is located 19 miles west of Krome Avenue (Southwest 177 Avenue) on Tamiami Trail (U.S. Highway 41) or 75 miles east of Naples. There is an entrance station, small visitor center and bookstore, and a concession that rents bicycles and operates a tram if you prefer to have a guided tour. Rangers and volunteers also offer guided walks.

Hours of Operation

The Shark Valley gate opens at 8:30 A.M. daily, and Shark Valley Visitor Center is open from 9:00 A.M. to 4:30 P.M. daily. The parking lot closes at 6:00 P.M., so be sure to plan your trip so that you arrive back before then. Entry before 8:30 A.M. or after 6:00 P.M. is allowed for walk-in visitors or bicyclists. There is no fee for entry before or after hours, but be sure to park outside of the posted NO PARKING signs at the park entrance or the Miccosukee police may issue you a parking ticket. Parking is not allowed close to the entrance because cars block the view at the intersection of Tamiami Trail and the park entrance.

Everglades National Park, Shark Valley

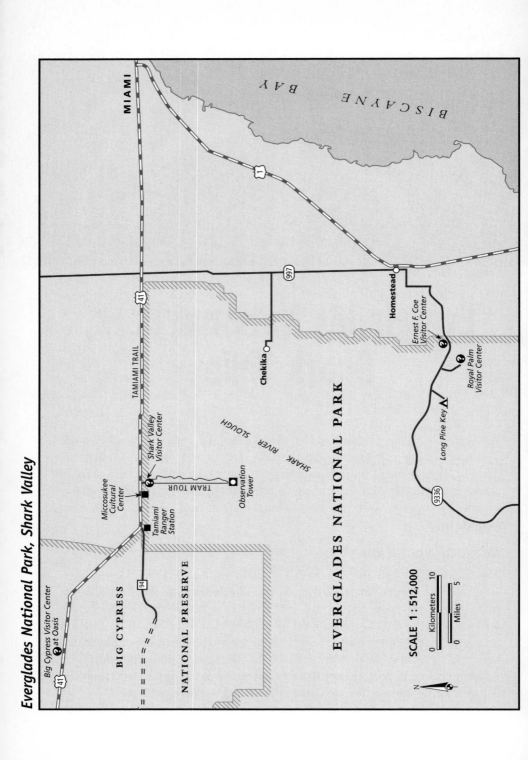

Entrance Fee

$10.00 per vehicle. Free entry if a pass holder is in the vehicle. Walk-in visitors, motorcyclists, and bicyclists are charged an entry fee of $5.00 per person.

Group Permits

Organized groups of twenty bicyclists or more must obtain a Special Use Permit prior to arrival at Shark Valley. Special Use Permits can be obtained by phoning (305) 225–3004 or (305) 221–8776. To request an application by mail, write to Fee Collection Supervisor, S.R. 42—Shark Valley, Everglades National Park, Ochopee, FL 34141. Allow two weeks for application processing and receipt of the permit.

Groups planning to bicycle Shark Valley after park hours must also have a Special Use Permit and are limited to no more than twenty-five participants.

Bike Rentals

Bicycles can be rented from a private concessionaire at Shark Valley. Rentals are available from 8:30 A.M. to 3:00 P.M., and all bikes must be returned by 4:00 P.M.

Motorized Tram

The guided tram tour is available all year, but times of operation vary with the season. From December through April the tram runs every hour on the hour from 9:00 A.M. until 4:00 P.M. From May through November tram rides are available at 9:30 and 11:00 A.M. and at 1:00 and 3:00 P.M. The tour takes about two hours. Current fees are $12.75 per adult and $7.75 for children age twelve and younger. Seniors (age sixty-two and older) are charged $11.75 per person but can enter the park free of charge with a Golden Age Pass available for a one-time fee of $10.00. Tram fees and bike-rental fees sometimes change from year to year, so phone or inquire in person for the current fees.

Safety

- Helmets are required by Florida law for children age sixteen and younger. Helmets can be purchased (not rented) at Shark Valley.

- Always maintain a safe speed on bicycles, not only for your safety and the safety of other bikers and hikers but also for the well-being of wildlife that might be crossing or lying on the trail. Although the speed limit for bicycles at Shark Valley is 25 miles per hour, it is much more enjoyable to travel at a leisurely pace and enjoy the wildlife, wildflowers, and scenery along the trail.

- Always hike and bike against the flow of tram traffic. The tram travels the trail in a clockwise direction, so hikers and bikers should travel up the straight paved trail that leads due north from the visitor center. This will allow you to see the trams coming and step off the trail. *You are required to come to a complete stop and step off to the right of the trail when a tram approaches.*

- Very large alligators sometimes lie on or near the trail. Give them a wide berth (at least 15 feet) when going around them. If this much room is not available, wait until it moves or wait until the tram comes along and frightens it off the trail. Remember too that it is unlawful to throw anything at alligators or otherwise harass them.

- Be sure to take plenty of water along on your trip, especially if you plan on completing the entire 15-mile loop. Sunscreen, mosquito repellent, and a hat are also advised.

About the Snail Kite

One of the must-see birds of the Everglades is the snail kite, and the area around Shark Valley is the best place to view this bird of prey in its natural habitat. If you are unable to locate any along the Shark Valley Trail, look north of the Miccosukee Indian restaurant along Tamiami Trail. Or travel three-quarters of a mile west of the Shark Valley entrance to the roadside parking area on the right. Scan the trees with binoculars or look for the birds soaring over the saw-grass as they seek their prey—apple snails *(Pomacea paludosa)*.

The upper beak of the snail kite is curved, which allows it to efficiently remove the snail from the shell. A mature apple snail is about the size of a golf ball, and unlike other mollusks, it must periodically come to the surface to breathe. This allows it to be seen by snail kites that fly back and forth over the shallow water. Because this is the only food the snail kite eats, its survival is completely dependent upon the health and abundance of apple snails. If you look closely, you may notice clusters of pea-sized white eggs of apple snails attached to emergent vegetation just above the water level.

In the early 1970s the population of the snail kite in Florida had declined to no more than thirty birds, but they are now more abundant. The Everglades restoration project currently under way will hopefully offer this special bird a chance to become even more common as water is brought back to historical levels across a broader area of the Everglades. Other Everglades animals that eat apple snails are alligators, limpkins, and otters.

TYPE OF TRAIL: Hiking, biking, or tram.

TYPE OF ADVENTURE: Hike, bike, or ride a tram on a paved trail though a vast Everglades marsh.

TOTAL DISTANCE: 15 miles round-trip.

DIFFICULTY: Easy to moderate on a bicycle, depending on wind speed and direction.

TIME REQUIRED: 2 to 3 hours or more.

SPECIAL CONCERNS: Mosquitoes and biting flies in summer and fall. Exposure. Large alligators sometimes lie on the trail.

SCENIC VALUE: Outstanding, especially from the observation tower at the end of the trail.

OVERVIEW AND TRAIL DESCRIPTION: The trailhead is right behind the visitor center. If you are a bird-watcher, you will want to hike or bike slowly, with frequent stops, to take in the variety of birds that can be seen here. Typical birds to look for include common moorhens, egrets, herons, anhingas, red-winged blackbirds, grackles, and red-shouldered hawks. Specialty birds that can be seen here are snail kites, wood storks, purple gallinules, least bitterns, American bitterns, limpkins, and rails. Black-crowned nightherons and yellow-crowned nightherons can also be seen here. Alligators are common along the trail and baby alligators can be seen seasonally, often crowded together in groups. Watch for a number of water snakes, including venomous cottonmouth moccasins, along with softshell turtles, mud turtles, sliders, and cooters. Fish abound in the canal along the trail, but not all of them are welcome. The aquarium trade and fish farms are responsible for the release of numerous exotic fish from around the world into southern Florida waters, and many of those species now reside permanently in the Everglades. Look for Mayan cichlids, oscars, walking catfish, and tilapia among the native largemouth bass, spotted gars, bluegills, and mudfish. Otters and even bobcats are sometimes seen at Shark Valley, so it's always a good idea to bike or hike slowly and quietly to give yourself the best chance of seeing these or other interesting, seldom-seen animals.

If you look closely you might see clusters of small white eggs stuck to emergent vegetation just above the water level. These belong to the apple snail, a large native aquatic snail that serves as food for otters, alligators, and snail kites. The beak of the snail kite is designed to be able to pull the animal from the shell with ease. Watch for this endangered bird of prey as it gracefully soars and then hovers over the freshwater marsh looking for apple snails.

Shark Valley Trail

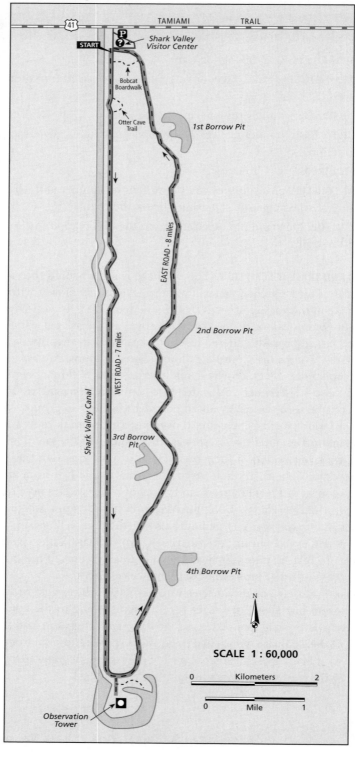

The first half of the trail is relatively straight and leads to a tall observation tower (restrooms available) where you can get a bird's-eye view of Shark Valley—a wide swath of saw-grass that channels water southwest to the Shark River and eventually into the Gulf of Mexico. This fresh water is vitally important for the health of biologically rich mangrove forests and estuaries of Florida's southwest coast. The tower is 7 miles from the trailhead. If you are completing the loop, the eastern half of the trail meanders past four "borrow pits," which are simply artificial ponds created when limestone was excavated to construct the elevated tram road. Although artificial, these ponds are habitat for a wide range of wildlife.

The tram offers a slow comfortable ride with frequent stops while interpreters identify wildlife and explain points of interest along the way. Interpreters are private concession employees, park rangers, or park volunteers. If you want a relaxing way to see Shark Valley, the tram is a good choice.

Bobcat Boardwalk

TYPE OF TRAIL: Walking.

TYPE OF ADVENTURE: Walk along a short boardwalk through a bayhead and low hardwood hammock.

TOTAL DISTANCE: 0.33 mile round-trip.

DIFFICULTY: Easy.

TIME REQUIRED: Half an hour.

SPECIAL CONCERNS: Mosquitoes and biting flies in summer and fall.

SCENIC VALUE: Good. This short trail allows viewing of some interesting tropical and temperate zone trees.

OVERVIEW AND TRAIL DESCRIPTION: The trailhead is just a short distance down the Shark Valley Trail on the left and is marked by signage. A common tree in this area is sweetbay *(Magnolia virginiana)*, which can easily be recognized by its leaves with silvery undersides and its showy, perfumed white flowers. You might also see its fruits, which split open to reveal bright red seeds. Another common tree seen here is redbay *(Persea borbonia)*. This tree is closely related to the avocado *(Persea americana)*, and it has very fragrant leaves that have been used for cooking, similar to the related, culinary bay leaf *(Laurus nobilis)*. The leaves of redbay are often deformed by the larvae of a small fly, almost to the point where the deformity becomes a means of identification.

Otter Cave Trail

TYPE OF TRAIL: Walking.

TYPE OF ADVENTURE: Walk along a trail that bisects a small hardwood hammock.

TOTAL DISTANCE: 0.25-mile loop back to the trailhead.

DIFFICULTY: Easy.

TIME REQUIRED: 20 minutes.

SPECIAL CONCERNS: Mosquitoes and biting flies in summer and fall. Watch for small natural holes in the trail.

SCENIC VALUE: Good. This trail leads through a small shady hardwood hammock with exposed limestone substrate and other natural features.

OVERVIEW AND TRAIL DESCRIPTION: The trailhead is on the left side of the Shark Valley Trail and loops back to the main paved trail. To continue to the observation tower, turn left once you are back on the Shark Valley Trail. This is a worthwhile diversion off the main trail to see different birds than you might see elsewhere at Shark Valley. Watch for warblers, vireos (black-whiskered vireos in late spring and summer), tanagers, flycatchers, gnatcatchers, and other resident and migratory birds. Lucky visitors might see otters or even bobcats.

Big Cypress National Preserve

Although the Big Cypress National Preserve is contiguous with Everglades National Park to the south and east, it is floristically much different. While the true Everglades are open watery prairies with a mosaic of hardwood hammocks, pine rocklands, mangroves, and other interrelated ecosystems, the Big Cypress National Preserve is characterized by a more temperate inventory of plants that make up the swamps, hammocks, pinelands, and prairies. Deep cypress sloughs and strands channel water south, and many of these are bisected by Tamiami Trail. A free brochure map of the preserve that shows the locations of the various sloughs, trails, and other points of interest is available at the Big Cypress Visitor Center at Oasis. If you are the adventurous type, stop at one of the sloughs and take a walk into the watery interior.

Unlike Everglades National Park, the Big Cypress National Preserve does not have an official entrance, nor is a fee charged to enter the preserve. Off-road hikes can be rewarding, exhilarating, and educational, so feel free to stop anywhere and explore—using common sense, of course. Read the Hazards and Health Warnings section in the Introduction before heading out on your wilderness adventure.

Big Cypress National Preserve

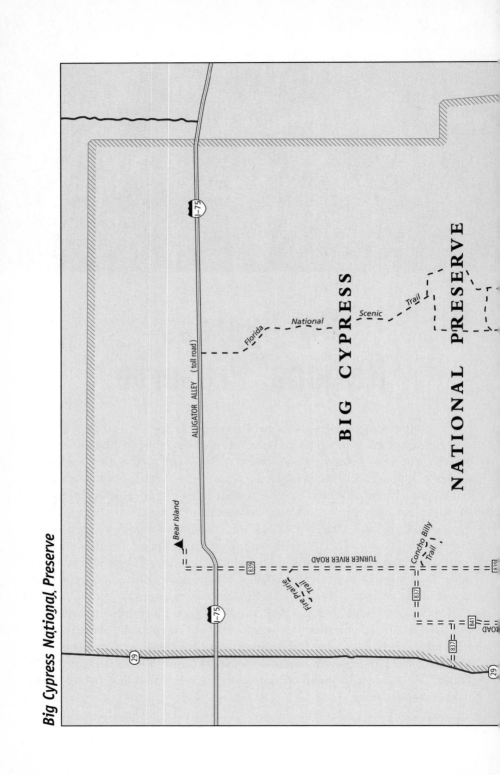

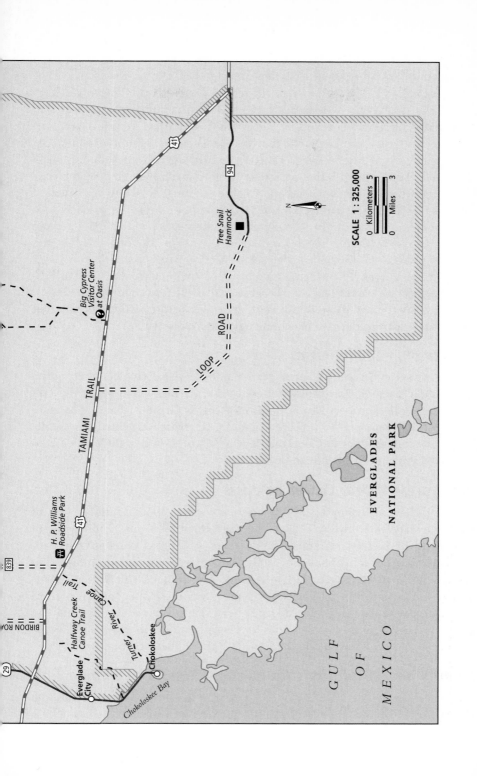

Big Cypress National Preserve falls under a different management plan than Everglades National Park. The preserve was protected by Congress in 1974 and expanded to 729,000 acres in 1988. Hunting and fishing are allowed, as are all-terrain vehicles (ATVs) and airboats. All-terrain vehicles (including swamp buggies, which are elevated homemade vehicles with extremely large tires that allow them to traverse relatively deep water and rough terrain) are now restricted to designated trails, and permits are issued by a lottery system. The unregulated use of swamp buggies throughout the years has resulted in many thousands of miles of trails that crisscross the preserve, leaving permanent damage in the form of deep ruts running in all directions. To see the destruction from the air is disheartening. Private land holdings within the preserve also allow hunters the legal right to build cabins and makeshift shelters in remote areas accessible by swamp buggies and other ATVs. The tires of swamp buggies leave deep ruts in the muck that adversely affect the natural water flow and even alter vegetation types. Their banning in parts of the Big Cypress National Preserve has been a contentious issue because of their historical unregulated use.

Oil exploration is allowed in certain areas due to preexisting permits that were issued prior to the area becoming a national preserve.

Surrounding Communities

The nearest city to the Big Cypress National Preserve is Everglades City at the northwest corner of Everglades National Park. Farther north along the gulf coast are Naples and Fort Myers, and to the east is Greater Miami. The main access road is Tamiami Trail (U.S. Highway 41), which bisects the preserve. The small communities of Copeland, Jerome, Carnestown, and Ochopee border the preserve on the south and west.

Big Cypress Visitor Center at Oasis

The Big Cypress Visitor Center at Oasis is located about 55 miles west of Krome Avenue (Southwest 177 Avenue; State Road 997) and 22 miles east of State Road 29 on Tamiami Trail. The Big Cypress Visitor Center at Oasis provides restrooms, a small bookstore, static wildlife exhibits, and an information desk staffed by park rangers and volunteers. The center also offers a fifteen-minute educational film about the Big Cypress Swamp. Hours of operation are 8:30 A.M. to 4:30 P.M. daily (closed December 25). Outside the Big Cypress Visitor Center at Oasis are opportunities for viewing wildlife in and around Tamiami Canal and for hiking along the Florida National Scenic Trail.

Permits and Regulations for Hiking, Biking, or Camping

A free backcountry permit is required if you plan to camp overnight within the Big Cypress National Preserve or to hike or bike on trails for the day. These permits are available at major trailheads or at the Big Cypress Visitor Center at Oasis. The information you provide allows the park rangers to gain valuable information regarding trail use and types of uses in the backcountry. The permit also provides information on your whereabouts so if you get lost or have a medical emergency, park rangers will have a much smaller area to search. Needless to say, the information on the permit could save your life. No permit is necessary if you just plan on stopping and exploring for a short period of time, but use common sense and bring plenty of water, a compass, and other supplies that you feel you may need. A walking stick is invaluable to keep from tripping and falling. Also make certain that you let rangers at the Big Cypress Visitor Center at Oasis know that you have made it safely back from your trip, so they don't think you are lost out there somewhere.

Hunting

Visitors to the Big Cypress National Preserve should be aware of hunting season and *always wear blaze orange hats, shirts, or vests* to avoid being mistaken for a deer or other game animal. Check at the Big Cypress Visitor Center at Oasis to find out which areas are safest to explore during hunting season, or to inquire about regulations regarding hunting and fishing in the preserve. Firearms are prohibited except with a valid hunting license during hunting season.

Off-Road Vehicles

Off-road vehicles (ORVs) are allowed only by permit within certain designated areas of the Big Cypress National Preserve. The Recreational Off-Road Vehicle Management Plan requires seasonal closure to ORVs (except landowners who have permits to access their private property) during a sixty-day ban from mid-June to mid-August each year. ORVs are destructive to plant communities and leave deep, permanent ruts in an otherwise pristine wilderness. ORV owners contend that swamp buggies were historically used to access the interior of the Big Cypress Swamp long before the area became a national preserve in 1974, and they should therefore be allowed. A compromise that restricts ORV use to designated areas is a part of the Recreational Off-Road Vehicle Management Plan recently approved by the National Park Service.

Safety Hazards

Most of the same safety hazards listed for Everglades National Park apply here as well. Cottonmouth moccasins are rather plentiful in the Big Cypress National Preserve, so be especially cautious when exploring watery areas where this venomous snake occurs. In the dry season they will be congregated around such areas of permanent water in strands and the deeper sloughs, alligator holes, and canals. Upland areas may harbor Eastern diamondback rattlesnakes and dusky pygmy rattlesnakes. The feral hog is another potentially dangerous animal to be aware of in this region. Although they will almost always run away when humans approach, hogs will defend their young if confronted. Unless you decide to explore rather remote areas, the likelihood of encountering feral hogs is slim. These are descendants of free-ranging swine introduced into Florida by Spanish explorers in the sixteenth century. Although they are somewhat destructive to natural vegetation, they now offer sport for hunters. They are a favorite prey of the endangered Florida panther as well.

Venomous snakes, alligators, and other potentially dangerous animals aside, the most hazardous aspect of exploring the Big Cypress National Preserve is driving on Tamiami Trail (US 41). This road is well known by locals as being dangerous due to speeding cars and trucks, so drive carefully.

If you plan on fishing in the Big Cypress National Preserve, be aware that many freshwater fish have high mercury content and are unsafe to eat on a frequent basis. Young children and pregnant women should avoid them altogether. Occasional signs are posted that warn anglers of the potential danger of eating fish from this region.

Know the symptoms of heat exhaustion and heat stroke and how to treat these potentially life-threatening health problems. Always bring more water than you think you will need, and always wear sunglasses, a wide-brimmed hat, and lightweight clothing if you are exploring or camping in summer.

Camping

There are six campgrounds in the Big Cypress National Preserve, and three are marked by signage along Tamiami Trail. All campsites are available on a first-come basis. Monument Lake Campground offers restrooms and potable water, but all others are currently primitive. All sites allow tent camping and most are accessible to motor homes and portable campers. There is a dump station and potable water at Dona Drive about a quarter of a mile east of Big Cypress Headquarters. One remote campground is located 20 miles north on the Turner River Road (County Road 839) in the Bear Island Unit. The turnoff to Turner River Road is at the H. P. Williams Roadside Park along Tamiami Trail about 15 miles west of the Big Cypress Visitor Center at Oasis or 7 miles east of SR 29.

U.S. Post Office—Ochopee, Florida

If you have not visited the U.S. Post Office in Ochopee, be sure to buy a postcard to mail, and bring your camera! The post office is 21.5 miles west of the Big Cypress Visitor Center at Oasis on Tamiami Trail (US 41) or 4 miles east of SR 29. The building measures only 7 feet 3 inches by 8 feet 4 inches and has the dubious distinction of being the smallest (and most photographed) U.S.

Once a tool shed, the Ochopee Post Office is easily the smallest and most photographed post office in the United States.

Post Office in the nation. The original Ochopee Post Office was established in 1932 and was located inside a general store at the site. When a fire burned the general store down in 1953, the tool shed in the back was moved closer to the road to serve as the local post office. It eventually became a landmark that still services the surrounding community.

Loop Road Scenic Drive (County Road 94)

TYPE OF TRAIL: Driving or biking.

TYPE OF ADVENTURE: Sightseeing by vehicle or bike on a paved road with opportunities to stop and explore on foot.

TOTAL DISTANCE: Approximately 16 miles.

DIFFICULTY: Easy in a vehicle, of course; easy to moderate on a bicycle.

TIME REQUIRED: 1 hour or more in a vehicle; all day on a bicycle.

SPECIAL CONCERNS: Potholes (mostly in the western half). Mosquitoes and biting flies can be problems in summer and fall if you are on a bicycle.

SCENIC VALUE: Excellent. The road traverses typical cypress and mixed-hardwood swamp habitat.

OVERVIEW AND TRAIL DESCRIPTION: Loop Road can be accessed by driving 5 miles west of Shark Valley on Tamiami Trail (US 41) to the Forty Mile Bend (turn left where Tamiami Trail turns northwest). The Tamiami Ranger Station is located at the turnoff. For those traveling east on Tamiami Trail, turn south at Monroe Station to access Loop Road.

Take your time because there are opportunities to see white-tailed deer, black bears, otters, feral hogs, and even endangered Florida panthers on or near the road (a good reason to drive slowly). The small village of Pinecrest offers a glimpse of home life for some very hardy people who got tired of city life and moved to this remote area to take up residence. Imagine living where the nearest town with a grocery store is more than an hour drive in either direction. It is definitely a no-frills lifestyle, but the people who chose it wouldn't give it up for anything. The eastern portion is now lined with homes built by Miccosukee Indians in once-pristine Everglades habitat, complete with satellite dishes and other modern amenities.

There is primitive camping available at the Pinecrest campsite (6 miles west of the eastern entrance to Loop Road off of Tamiami Trail). This campsite is on the north side of Loop Road. The Mitchell Landing campsite is 1 mile farther west on the south side of Loop Road. Two miles farther west is the Loop Road Education Center (about 9 miles west of Tamiami Trail) where there is a short

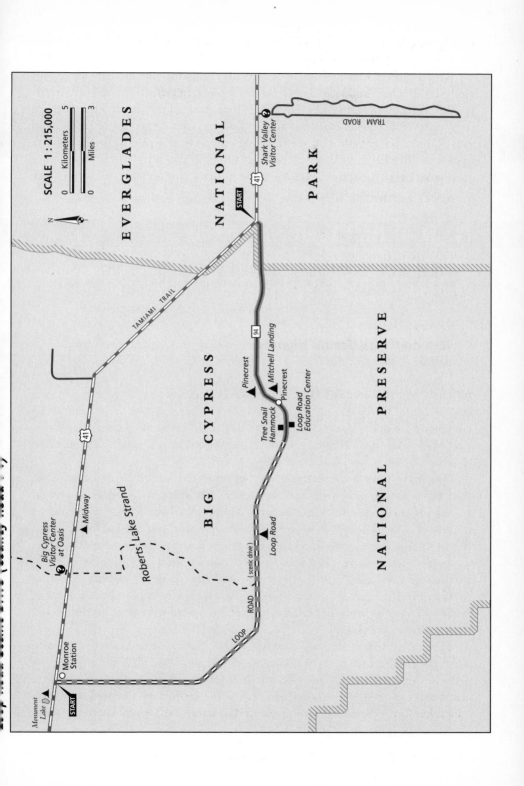

SCALE 1:215,000

N

Kilometers
0   5

Miles
0   3

EVERGLADES

NATIONAL

PARK

Shark Valley
Visitor Center

TRAM ROAD

41

START

94

Pinecrest

Mitchell Landing

Pinecrest

Tree Snail
Hammock

Loop Road
Education Center

TAMIAMI TRAIL

BIG   CYPRESS

NATIONAL   PRESERVE

Loop Road
(scenic drive)

LOOP   ROAD

Roberts Lake Strand

Big Cypress
Visitor Center
at Oasis

Midway

41

Monroe
Station

START

Monument
Lake

hiking trail on the north side of Loop Road that is worth exploring. It is called the Tree Snail Hammock Trail.

Watch for interesting birds—especially limpkins—while driving slowly along Loop Road, and keep an eye out for snakes, turtles, frogs, and other critters on the road or in the adjacent canal along parts of the drive. The southern terminus of the Florida National Scenic Trail can be accessed off of Loop Road as well. Take note that if you are traveling east to west on Loop Road, you will bypass the Big Cypress Visitor Center at Oasis. If you want to visit the center after your Loop Road tour, you will have to drive east about 4 miles once you get back on Tamiami Trail.

Tamiami Trail Scenic Highway

TYPE OF TRAIL: Sightseeing by automobile with opportunities to stop and explore on foot. Biking is especially dangerous and is not recommended.

Tamiami Trail Scenic Highway

TYPE OF ADVENTURE: Drive along a designated scenic highway through the Big Cypress National Preserve to Collier-Seminole State Park.

TOTAL DISTANCE: 50 miles.

TIME REQUIRED: 3 to 4 hours for sightseeing.

SPECIAL CONCERNS: Dangerously fast traffic. Do not drive too slowly and never stop in the travel lanes. If you decide to pull off the roadway, do so on the south side where there is a wide swale. Use your turn signals and allow plenty of time to pull over. Also be especially careful when crossing Tamiami Trail on foot. Always stand on the opposite side of the guardrail between the road and Tamiami Canal on the north side of the road when viewing wildlife in or near the canal.

SCENIC VALUE: Excellent. This scenic highway bisects cypress strand and mixed-hardwood swamp habitats that are periodically interrupted by open, sunny prairies.

OVERVIEW AND TRAIL DESCRIPTION: The Tamiami Trail Scenic Highway begins in the east at the Forty Mile Bend as you exit the Miccosukee Indian Reservation and continues west through the Big Cypress National Preserve to Collier-

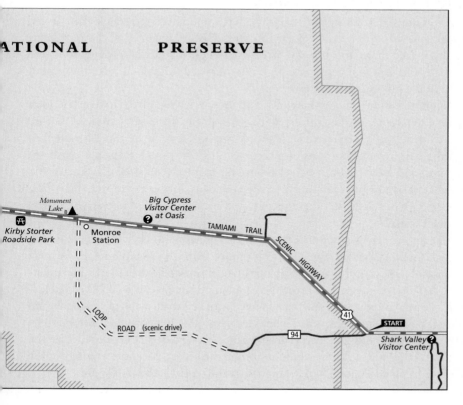

Clyde Butcher's Big Cypress Gallery

Located 55 miles west of Krome Avenue (Southwest 177 Avenue) on Tamiami Trail, or about 22 miles east of SR 29, is the Big Cypress Gallery, owned by renowned photographer Clyde Butcher. A large selection of his black-and-white photographs can be seen or purchased at his gallery. His award-winning images are created using large-format view cameras that allow him to capture incredible detail and textures of the natural Florida landscape. His photographs are available in sizes ranging from 16 by 20 inches to 5 by 9 feet. Large original images can sell for more than $20,000, and his photography is often displayed in such public places as museums, government offices, and national parks. If you are just browsing or looking to buy a lifetime reminder of your visit to Florida, a stop at the Big Cypress Gallery is definitely worthwhile.

Seminole State Park. It is regarded as one of the most scenic highways in Florida. Tamiami Trail was completed in 1928, and its name was taken from the two cities it connected—Tampa and Miami. The National Scenic Byways Program recognizes highways nationwide that are "outstanding examples of our nation's beauty, history, culture, and recreational experience by designating them as All-American Roads and National Scenic Byways."

An abundance of wildlife, including birds, alligators, otters, snakes, frogs, turtles, and fish, can be seen along this stretch of Tamiami Trail. Even though this is a scenic drive, it cannot be stressed enough that it is also dangerous due to trucks and cars that travel at a high rate of speed (often well over the posted speed limit). So use extreme caution.

There are bridges along this route, and these are good places to stop and look for fish, alligators, turtles, otters, and wading birds. Fishing is allowed, but be sure to read the Hazards and Health Warnings section in the Introduction regarding high concentrations of mercury in the fish of this region. Garfish are plentiful, and alligators can be seen sunning themselves along the canal bank. Wood storks and egrets can be especially abundant during the winter and spring dry season when fish become concentrated in permanently wet areas such as Tamiami Canal.

The cypress trees along this route are festooned with bromeliads, including Spanish moss (*Tillandsia usneoides*) that drapes from the tree branches. Spanish moss is not a moss, nor is it from Spain. It is the most widespread of all bromeliads, but is also the most non-bromeliad-looking bromeliad as well. The big clustering bromeliad adorning the trees in mass is the cardinal airplant or stiff-leaved wild-pine (*Tillandsia fasciculata*). This species produces a branched flower spike covered with red and greenish yellow bracts. You have to get up close to see the narrow tubular purple flowers hidden among the bracts. As a note of interest, the most well-known (and edible) bromeliad in the world is the pineapple.

You will be traversing the Big Cypress National Preserve so be sure to familiarize yourself with trails in this region. Remember too that there are ample opportunities to stop anywhere along the way for some adventurous off-trail exploring. A compass is advisable if you decide to hike very far. The open prairies can harbor an abundance of wildflowers, especially if the prairies have burned recently.

Florida National Scenic Trail (Northern Big Cypress Section)

TYPE OF TRAIL: Hiking.

TYPE OF ADVENTURE: Hike along a marked trail through prairie, pineland, sloughs, and cypress forests.

TOTAL DISTANCE: Varies; hiking from the Big Cypress Visitor Center at Oasis to the rest area at Alligator Alley (Interstate75) is either 40 miles one way or 28 miles one way, depending on which side of the loop portion of the trail you take (the east side is the longer route). A southern extension of the trail between Tamiami Trail and Loop Road is an additional 8 miles one way. The trail is also accessible about 18 miles east of SR 29 at a rest area along Alligator Alley (I–75; toll road).

DIFFICULTY: Moderate to strenuous; most difficult in summer due to troublesome mosquitoes, flooding, and sweltering heat. Expect muddy areas or standing water during the summer and fall, or after rains anytime of the year.

TIME REQUIRED: Varies; 4 days to complete the trail round-trip.

SPECIAL CONCERNS: Mosquitoes and biting flies in summer and fall. Remember that you are in a wilderness area that may include encounters with venomous snakes and other wildlife.

SCENIC VALUE: Excellent once you hike past the National Park Service airport facilities north of the Big Cypress Visitor Center at Oasis.

OVERVIEW AND TRAIL DESCRIPTION: The trailhead begins at the west side of the Big Cypress Visitor Center at Oasis parking lot, first paralleling Tamiami Canal westward and then turning north. Swamp buggies have created deep ruts in the first several hundred yards of the trail, so this area can be mucky during the wet season. Once you cross the first prairie, the trail becomes much more scenic and enjoyable. Primitive tent camping is available at two designated sites along the trail. The first campsite is 7 miles from the trailhead, and the second campsite is an additional 10-mile hike. Members of the Florida Trail Association blaze

Florida National Scenic Trail (Northern Big Cypress Section)

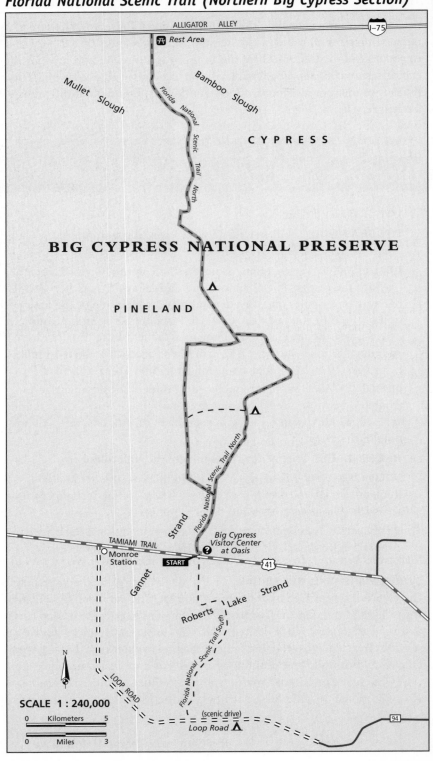

ALLIGATOR   ALLEY

I-75

Rest Area

Mullet Slough

Bamboo Slough

Florida National Scenic Trail North

CYPRESS

BIG CYPRESS NATIONAL PRESERVE

PINELAND

Florida National Scenic Trail North

TAMIAMI TRAIL

Strand

Big Cypress
Visitor Center
at Oasis

Monroe
Station

START

41

Gannet

Roberts   Lake   Strand

Florida National Scenic Trail South

N

LOOP ROAD

SCALE 1 : 240,000

0   Kilometers   5

0   Miles   3

(scenic drive)
Loop Road

94

trees to help designate the official trail, but exploring off-trail is allowed. Be sure to have a compass or GPS unit if you decide to explore off-trail.

Before beginning your wilderness adventure, inquire about the trail conditions at the Big Cypress Visitor Center at Oasis. Rangers and volunteers at the front desk can answer any pertinent questions and offer firsthand advice. Bring plenty of water, even if you are only hiking a portion of the trail.

This can be a short or long hike, depending on your intent and skills. A 13-mile loop is available by hiking to the first campsite and then taking the trail to the west until it bisects another trail. Turn back south to complete the loop. You can, of course, simply turn around and go back at any time, but it is well worth the effort to at least get far enough away so you no longer see buildings and hear traffic.

Wildflowers can be abundant at times, and if you are lucky enough to walk the trail in early summer, you will

Explorers lucky enough to hike into the vast prairies of the Big Cypress National Preserve in late spring and summer will be greeted by hundreds of blossoms of Bartram's rosegentian (Sabatia bartramii).

be rewarded with hundreds of eye-catching pink blossoms of Bartram's rosegentian *(Sabatia bartramii),* named to honor the intrepid explorer William Bartram (1739–1823). Bartram traveled through Florida and was the first native-born American to spend his life as a naturalist. From March to May the wet sunny prairies are adorned with two spring-flowering terrestrial orchids, the grass-pink *(Calopogon tuberosus* var. *simpsonii)* and the spring ladies' tresses *(Spiranthes vernalis).* In early summer you can also see the snowy orchid *(Platanthera nivea),* with interesting snow-white blossoms that smell like grape jam.

Hiking the length of the Florida National Scenic Trail from Tamiami Trail to Alligator Alley requires staying at either of the campsites along the way, and it is not a trail to underestimate. Backpacking with a load of camping gear and provisions can be very strenuous, so consider the length of this trail and your skills as a hiker before embarking on your journey.

Florida National Scenic Trail (Southern Big Cypress Section)

TYPE OF TRAIL: Hiking.

TYPE OF ADVENTURE: Hike along a marked trail through cypress forests, pineland, sloughs, and prairies.

TOTAL DISTANCE: 8.25 miles one way.

DIFFICULTY: Moderate to strenuous.

TIME REQUIRED: All day to complete the trail round-trip.

SPECIAL CONCERNS: Mosquitoes and biting flies in summer and fall. Uneven trail can be slippery when muddy or flooded.

SCENIC VALUE: Excellent. This is a scenic trail that is seldom traveled. If you are looking for solitude in a pristine area with good bird-watching opportunities, then this trail is well worthwhile.

OVERVIEW AND TRAIL DESCRIPTION: The trailhead for this portion of the Florida National Scenic Trail is located directly across Tamiami Trail (US 41) from the Big Cypress Visitor Center at Oasis and terminates at Loop Road 8.25 miles to the south (or begin on Loop Road and hike north). It is easier to hike this trail during the dry season, but it is more interesting and refreshing to hike when the trail is flooded. Water levels may range from ankle- to knee-deep, unless you decide to sidetrack into one of the deep sloughs where the water may be waist-deep or more. The trail can be a loop if you hike back west and then north on Loop Road to Tamiami Trail and then back east to the Big Cypress Visitor Center at Oasis. At the intersection of Tamiami Trail and the western intersection of Loop Road is Monroe Station, which was once a lively hangout for hunters and locals and the site of an annual wild-hog barbecue. It closed in the 1990s.

Off-road vehicles are not allowed in the area enclosed by Loop Road and Tamiami Trail, but hunting is allowed. This southern portion of the Florida National Scenic Trail bisects Roberts Lake Strand, which is one of the most scenic and interesting cypress strands in the Big Cypress National Preserve. Note that the trail turns east-west at Roberts Lake Strand but then veers back north-south. Take your time and look for unusual epiphytes (ferns, bromeliads, orchids, peperomias) growing on the trees, a variety of birds, and even the occasional mammal, reptile, or amphibian to make your hike interesting and memorable. If you find that you have lost the trail (or it lost you!), use your compass or GPS to continue on a due north or south heading (depending, of course, on which direction you are hiking). North leads you back to Tamiami Trail and south will take you to Loop Road.

Florida National Scenic Trail (Southern Big Cypress Section)

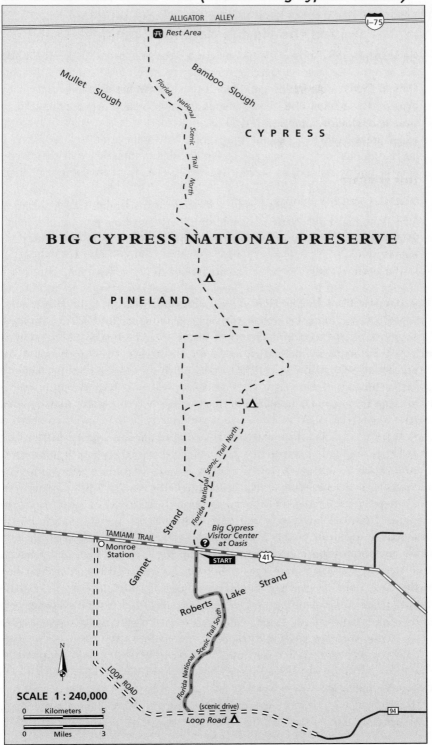

ALLIGATOR ALLEY

I-75

Rest Area

Mullet Slough

Bamboo Slough

Florida National Scenic Trail North

CYPRESS

BIG CYPRESS NATIONAL PRESERVE

PINELAND

Florida National Scenic Trail North

TAMIAMI TRAIL

Strand

Monroe Station

Gannet Strand

Big Cypress Visitor Center at Oasis

41

START

Lake Strand

Roberts

Florida National Scenic Trail South

N

LOOP ROAD

SCALE 1 : 240,000

| 0 | Kilometers | 5 |

| 0 | Miles | 3 |

(scenic drive)

Loop Road

94

About the Florida Trail Association and the Florida National Scenic Trail

Members of the Florida Trail Association help maintain the Florida National Scenic Trail. The association currently has seventeen local chapters throughout Florida. Each chapter holds monthly meetings for fellowship and educational programs, and to plan and coordinate group-sponsored hikes, paddling trips, or trail-maintenance activities. If you are new to Florida and wish to learn more about areas to hike or explore, the Florida Trail Association is a rewarding outlet for information and camaraderie. For detailed information visit their Web site at www.florida-trail.org or phone (877) HIKE–FLA. You can also e-mail them at fta@florida-trail.org.

Although you do not need to be a member of the Florida Trail Association to hike along the Florida National Scenic Trail, portions of the trail lead through private property and membership is a legal requirement to cross these private land holdings.

The entire Florida National Scenic Trail is 1,300 miles long, but this may change from year to year as the Florida Trail Association works to move portions of the trail off of private lands and away from roadways by relocating it through publicly owned natural corridors as they become available. Check the Florida Trail Association's Web site for "Notices to Hikers" or subscribe to their online mailing list for updated information on routes and access. The Florida Trail Association offers an End-to-End certificate and patch for members who complete the entire Florida National Scenic Trail. To qualify you must hike the entire trail as it exists at the time of your hike, and this includes portions of the trail along roadways (no hitchhiking!).

At least thirty days before departure, you are required to notify the Florida Trail Association of your intent to thru-hike. You must supply the association with such information as an address, phone number, emergency contact, and your proposed day-to-day itinerary. This is required because the Florida Trail Association must notify private landowners of the date and time hikers are expected to cross their property (private landowners may change their access policies at any time). As a courtesy to future hikers, respect private and public property at all times. You will be crossing portions of the Seminole Indian Reservation and federal property (Eglin Air Force Base), so you must have a letter with you from the Florida Trail Association in case you are stopped and questioned (do not carry firearms). Permits are required for portions of the trail—check out "Permits Needed to Hike the Florida Trail" on the Florida Trail Association's Web site. Be sure you acquire all of the pertinent maps and the book *Florida Trail—the Companion Guide for Long Distance Hikers* from the Florida Trail Association. The book contains information on campsites, water sources, nearby towns, post offices, and other pertinent information. Maps of the Florida National Scenic Trail are available at the Florida Trail Association's main office in Gainesville or through the Florida Trail Association's online store on their Web site. Happy hiking!

Endangered Florida panthers frequent this area, so even a fleeting glimpse of this magnificent feline predator will be one of those special moments that will linger in your mind for a lifetime. Bobcats, river otters, feral hogs, white-tailed deer, and Florida black bears are possible to see as well.

Turner River Road Scenic Drive

TYPE OF TRAIL: Driving, hiking, or biking.

TYPE OF ADVENTURE: Drive, hike, or bike along a graded dirt road that bisects a variety of habitats, including mixed-hardwood forests, cypress strands, prairies, and pineland. A canal borders the road on the east side.

TOTAL DISTANCE: 20 miles one way.

DIFFICULTY: Easy to moderate, depending on your mode of travel.

TIME REQUIRED: 2 hours by car.

SPECIAL CONCERNS: The road is very dusty during the dry season and is sometimes filled with potholes. It is graded periodically throughout the year to help keep it smooth for vehicle traffic. Proceed slowly and with caution. Be courteous and slow down when approaching parked vehicles and people, especially when the roadway is dusty. There are private land holdings along this road as well, so please respect private property.

SCENIC VALUE: Excellent. This can be a very rewarding sightseeing trip. Some of the views are outstanding, and wildlife abounds in and around the canal during most of the year. It is best during low water when wildlife congregates around deeper, and more permanent, water sources.

OVERVIEW AND TRAIL DESCRIPTION: Turner River Road (CR 839) begins at the H. P. Williams Roadside Park along Tamiami Trail. It terminates 20 miles to the north at the Bear Island Unit of Big Cypress National Preserve. There are a number of options when traveling this scenic road. There is a turnoff onto County Road 837 that leads west to Birdon Road (County Road 841). Birdon Road continues south back to Tamiami Trail, or you can turn west off of Birdon Road onto Wagonwheel Road (CR 837) to access SR 29. Be advised that there is no access from Turner River Road onto Alligator Alley (I–75).

Sightseeing from your car with periodic stops along the way is a popular venue for tourists and locals that drive this road. The canal that borders the road can be lively with alligators, otters, wading birds, ducks, and sometimes hundreds of swallows that swarm down en masse to sip water on the wing. If

Turner River Road Scenic Drive

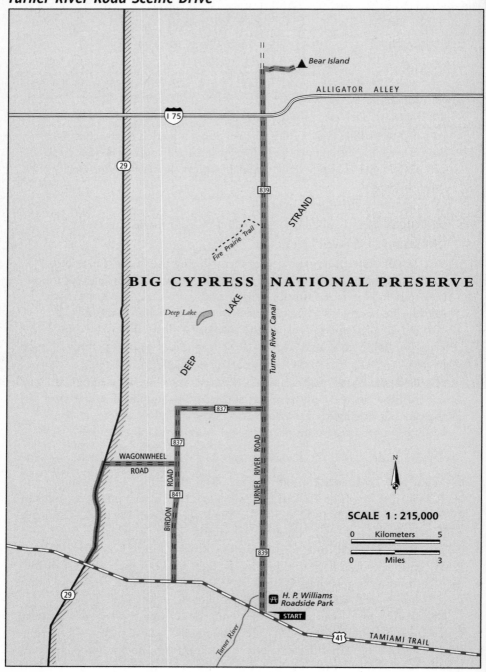

Bear Island

ALLIGATOR ALLEY

I 75

29

839

STRAND

Fire Prairie Trail

BIG CYPRESS NATIONAL PRESERVE

LAKE

Deep Lake

Turner River Canal

DEEP

837

837

WAGONWHEEL ROAD

BIRDON ROAD

841

TURNER RIVER ROAD

N

SCALE 1 : 215,000

0   Kilometers   5

0   Miles   3

839

H. P. Williams Roadside Park

START

29

Turner River

41   TAMIAMI TRAIL

Mixed-hardwood swamps and cypress forests can be seen along the Turner River Road in the Big Cypress National Preserve.

you are a reptile enthusiast, snakes occasionally cross this road, including venomous Eastern diamondback rattlesnakes, dusky pygmy rattlesnakes, and cottonmouth moccasins. The mud snake can also be seen at times. This is one of Florida's prettiest snakes. Adults are glossy jet black with a bright red belly and sides. Although it is an aquatic snake, it does cross roads, especially on rainy nights. If there is a hard rain that floods the canal and parts of the road, don't be surprised to see walking catfish hobbling on their fins from one side of the road to the other. This Asian catfish was inadvertently released into southern Florida waters by the aquarium trade and is now well-established in man-made canals and natural waterways throughout much of the Everglades region. To see a fish crossing the road is a bizarre sight.

Turner River Road can be a good biking adventure too, but parts of the road can be rough (sometimes like a washboard) if it has not been graded recently. The road is very dusty during the dry season, and airborne dust from passing cars can make hiking or biking poor choices of travel. Check the dust situation before you make any decisions to hike or bike along this road.

There are two side trails accessible from Turner River Road. The east trail is the Concho Billy Trail. This trail has been degraded by off-road vehicle use and currently is not recommended by the National Park Service for hiking or biking. The west trail is called the Fire Prairie Trail and is a 5-mile round-trip. This is an elevated trail, so it is usually dry when the surrounding habitats are wet. The trailhead for the Fire Prairie Trail is 14 miles north of Tamiami Trail on the west side of Turner River Road and is available for hiking or biking.

Bear Island Trails

TYPE OF TRAIL: Hiking or biking.

TYPE OF ADVENTURE: Hike or bike on dirt trails that traverse upland and wetland habitats.

TOTAL DISTANCE: Varies.

DIFFICULTY: Moderate.

TIME REQUIRED: Varies.

SPECIAL CONCERNS: Mosquitoes and biting flies in summer and fall. Hunters and off-road vehicles during hunting season.

SCENIC VALUE: Excellent. These trails crisscross through pristine native habitats and offer scenic vistas, bird-watching opportunities, and an abundance of flowering native plants to observe.

OVERVIEW AND TRAIL DESCRIPTION: The Bear Island Unit is accessible off the Turner River Road 20 miles north of Tamiami Trail. Turn right about 2 miles north of the I–75 overpass (no access from Turner River Road) and proceed east about 1 mile to the parking and camping areas. Camping is on a first-come basis, and there are no facilities. For safety let the rangers at the Big Cypress Visitor Center at Oasis know how long you plan on camping in the area. During hunting season there is a manned wildlife check station on your way in and out of the Bear Island Unit. If you plan on hiking or biking the trails during hunting season, be sure to wear bright orange or red clothing, hat, or vest as a safety precaution.

The trails in this region were created by off-road vehicles and are still used by them, so step off to the side of the trail when one approaches. Hunters and rangers know the Bear Island Unit trails better than anyone else, so they are a good source of information if you need local advice. Indeed, other than hunters and patrolling rangers, tourists or even most local visitors to the Big Cypress seldom use these trails. This is principally because the trails are not advertised to the general public as a destination, nor are they even marked on the Big Cypress brochure map. This does not mean that this region is off-limits or not worthwhile. If you're looking for adventure in a remote wilderness setting, or you want to camp in relative solitude, the Bear Island Unit is definitely worth the bumpy and sometimes dusty drive to get there.

There is an open parking area on your right just before the road ends. Camping areas are nothing more than cleared land and are mostly indicated by remnants of past campfires. The main trail leads north from the parking area and there are numerous side trails and loops, so keep track of which turns you have made. Some of the interesting animals that live in this region are Florida panthers, Florida black bear, white-tailed deer, feral hogs, river otters, hispid cotton rats, raccoons, opossum, Eastern gray squirrels, fox squirrels, and southern flying squirrels. Birds abound and there is a chance to see red-cockaded woodpeckers, pileated woodpeckers, brown-headed nuthatches, Eastern bluebirds, wild turkeys, swallow-tailed kites, bald eagles, barred owls, great horned owls, and a host of other species. American robins are common in the winter months along with other migratory species.

If you're lucky enough to be in this region in April or May, the many-flowered grass-pink *(Calopogon multiflorus)* can be found here, especially if a fire has burned through the habitat the previous summer or fall. This beautiful terrestrial orchid is on the southern extreme of its range in the Bear Island Unit and was only discovered there in 2000. There are also such interesting species as blackberries *(Rubus* spp.), shining blueberry *(Vaccinium myrsinites)*, wild pennyroyal *(Piloblephis rigida)*, and netted pawpaw *(Asimina reticulata)*. If you're a butterfly enthusiast, keep your eye out for zebra swallowtails, palamedes swallowtails, viceroys, and other interesting species. If you decide to explore off the trails through saw palmettos or around wet areas, be cautious of Eastern diamondback rattlesnakes and cottonmouth moccasins. And, speaking of wet areas, some trails in the Bear Island Unit can be flooded during the wet season of summer into fall.

Turner River and Halfway Creek Canoe Trails

TYPE OF TRAIL: Canoeing or kayaking.

TYPE OF ADVENTURE: Canoe or kayak along mangrove-lined creeks with the option of paddling to Chokoloskee Bay, Chokoloskee Island, Everglades City, or the Ten Thousand Islands.

TOTAL DISTANCE: 8 miles from the Turner River trailhead to Chokoloskee Island; about 6 miles from the Halfway Creek trailhead to the Chokoloskee causeway or to the Gulf Coast Visitor Center.

Turner River and Halfway Creek Canoe Trails

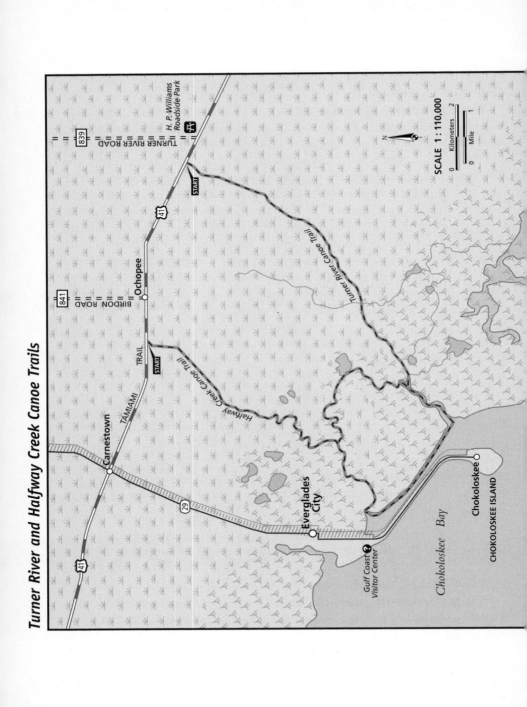

H. P. Williams
Roadside Park

839 TURNER RIVER ROAD

START

411

Ochopee

841 BIRDON ROAD

TAMIAMI   TRAIL

START

Turner River Canoe Trail

Halfway Creek Canoe Trail

Carnestown

411

29

Everglades
City

Gulf Coast
Visitor Center

Chokoloskee Bay

Chokoloskee

CHOKOLOSKEE ISLAND

N

SCALE 1 : 110,000

0   Kilometers   2

0   Mile   1

NAUTICAL CHARTS: NOAA Chart #11430 (Lostmans River to Wiggins Pass); Waterproof Chart #41 (Everglades & Ten Thousand Islands), although the scale on the waterproof chart is too small to be of much use for navigation; National Geographic Trails Illustrated Chart #243 (Everglades National Park), although not very detailed.

DIFFICULTY: Moderate to difficult, depending on wind and tides.

TIME REQUIRED: 5 to 6 hours or more.

SPECIAL CONCERNS: Mosquitoes and biting flies in summer and fall. Tides and wind can make paddling a strenuous ordeal at times, especially in the open waters of Chokoloskee Bay. Parts of these trails may be impassable during low tide in the dry season.

SCENIC VALUE: Good to excellent. The Turner River meanders through freshwater marsh and mangrove habitat and Halfway Creek traverses mangrove habitat. Both trails are scenic and offer access to the Ten Thousand Islands and Chokoloskee Island.

OVERVIEW AND TRAIL DESCRIPTION: These trails are combined because they connect to one another and the trailheads are only 4 miles apart. The Turner River Canoe Trail is accessible off of Tamiami Trail (US 41) and is a relatively straight creek that begins in a beautiful freshwater marsh and then enters brackish water mangrove habitat. If you have two vehicles, you can offload your canoes or kayaks at the Turner River trailhead and then take both vehicles to the Halfway Creek trailhead (or vice versa), returning in the other vehicle. This will allow your party to paddle a 13- to 14-mile loop or a 16- to 17-mile loop by connecting the two trails. Note that a new canoe launch into the Turner River is currently under construction on the north side of Tamiami Trail. The turnoff to the right after paddling 6 miles along the Turner River Trail is the shorter route. This creek is shaped like an upside down U and will lead you to Halfway Creek; turn right and the creek will terminate at the Halfway Creek trailhead along Seagrape Drive. A longer loop is possible by continuing along the Turner River Trail to Chokoloskee Bay, turning right and hugging the shoreline until you reach the entrance back into Halfway Creek, and then turning right (north) into the creek. Be advised that the last option requires you to paddle 2.5 miles in an open bay. If winds are strong, especially from the west or southwest, waves can be rough for a canoe.

The trailhead for the Halfway Creek Canoe Trail is located along Seagrape Drive. Seagrape Drive is next to the Big Cypress National Preserve Headquarters 1 mile west of the intersection of Tamiami Trail (US 41) and Birdon Road (CR 841), or 2.25 miles east of the intersection of Tamiami Trail and SR 29. Again, this trail can be looped back to the Turner River Trail or it can be a one-way trail that terminates either at the causeway leading to Chokoloskee Island or at the boat ramp near the Gulf Coast Visitor Center. You will have to arrange vehicle transport back to the trailhead if you take this route.

Both of these trails can be impassable in the dry season, especially at low tide, and also especially at a low tide around a full or new moon. It is advisable to check with the rangers at the Big Cypress Visitor Center at Oasis or Gulf Coast Visitor Center, either in person or in advance by phone, to see if these trails are passable.

Fakahatchee Strand Preserve State Park

The entrance to the Fakahatchee Strand Preserve State Park is located 2.5 miles north of Tamiami Trail (U.S. Highway 41) on State Route 29. Turn west at the sign for W. J. Janes Memorial Scenic Drive (County Road 837 West), and then bear right to reach the ranger station a short distance north on your right. Janes Memorial Scenic Drive is 11 miles one way and is a graded dirt road that is closed to vehicle traffic from sunset to 8:00 A.M. daily. It is, indeed, a scenic drive but if you do nothing more than drive its length, you will have missed the opportunity to see firsthand one of the real gems of the award-winning Florida state park system. If you are looking for real wild Florida, this is it. The Fakahatchee Strand was logged into the 1950s, and a complex network of elevated tram roads crisscross the swamp. These were built to allow cypress trunks to be hauled out of the swamp by small trains. Fortunately for the state of Florida—its residents, visitors, wildlife, and rare flora—the 80,000-acre Fakahatchee Strand was purchased for preservation in 1974, the same year the Big Cypress Swamp became a national preserve. The Fakahatchee Strand is a linear drainage system that channels fresh water from the Okaloacoochee Slough into the Ten Thousand Islands region along the Gulf of Mexico. It is literally a forested river.

Fakahatchee Strand Preserve State Park

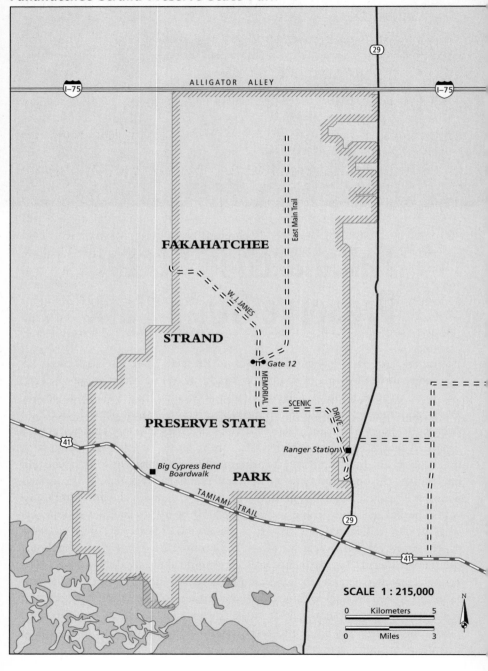

Some of the now-defunct tram roads have been cleared and offer easy access into the interior of the swamp. Botanically, this swamp is the crown jewel of Florida. Impressive numbers of native orchids, ferns, and bromeliads grace the swamp, and some are among the rarest plants in Florida. A few of the extremely rare species are the moss orchid (*Cranichis muscosa*), hanging club moss (*Lycopodium dichotomum*), tiny orchid (*Lepanthopsis melanantha*), purple tiger orchid (*Maxillaria parviflora*), yerba linda (*Peperomia rotundifolia*), cypress peperomia (*Peperomia glabella*), and dwarf butterfly orchid (*Prosthechea pygmaea*). Some are terrestrial, growing in the ground like normal plants, but many are epiphytic, adapted to growing on trees to gain access to better light conditions and to take advantage of a niche not available to other plants. Some trees are veritable air gardens of epiphytic plants.

And the Fakahatchee Swamp is not only a botanical paradise, it is home to many rare animals as well. Here your footprints can mingle with those of Florida panthers, Florida black bears, and Everglades mink. All of these animals occasionally can be sighted crossing Janes Memorial Scenic Drive, the main road leading through the preserve. Springtime is the best season to see Everglades mink, and they look like small weasels with a lopping gait. They are voracious hunters that eat crayfish, snakes, and amphibians, but they also will attack marsh rabbits and other mammals that outweigh them. If you should see one cross the road while driving, biking, or hiking, stop and be perfectly quiet and it will very likely come back out. Florida panthers are rarely seen, and many sightings turn out to be the smaller and less timid bobcat. Florida panthers are tawny colored with a long tail, unlike the bobcat, which is smaller and has a stubby tail.

Birdlife in the Fakahatchee Swamp is amazing, so be sure to bring binoculars. Here you can see common resident birds along with a wide array of rare or migratory species. During the late winter and spring dry season, fish become concentrated in deeper areas, such as roadside canals, and this bounty of food attracts wading birds such as herons, egrets, and wood storks that show up in large numbers to take advantage of the feeding opportunity. Colorful wood ducks and purple gallinules also frequent the canal along Janes Memorial Scenic Drive. Travel slowly so you don't miss anything and out of courtesy to hikers, bikers, and wildlife that may dart across the road. Don't let a road-killed animal be a memory of your visit.

Also be aware that cottonmouth moccasins are abundant in the Fakahatchee Swamp. It is wise to step with caution, especially if you are traveling off-trail in the interior of the swamp. Cottonmouth moccasins are belligerent, meaning they often hold their ground when approached (they don't "attack" people), and they are well camouflaged. Stepping on one and being bitten is a serious medical emergency. Return the victim to the ranger station as quickly as possible to

The deep sloughs in the interior of the Fakahatchee Strand in Collier County are among the prettiest and most botanically interesting habitats in Florida.

seek medical attention. If all of this sounds too intimidating, try to put the danger of venomous snakebite in perspective; there is an average of ninety-three lightning-caused deaths in the United States each year, and your chance of being struck by lightning is 576,000 to 1. People killed by venomous snakebite in the United States average fewer than twelve each year. Therefore, your chances of being struck by lightning are far greater than your chances of getting bitten by a venomous snake, if that makes you feel any better.

East Main Trail (Gate 12)

TYPE OF TRAIL: Hiking or biking.

TYPE OF ADVENTURE: Hike or bike along a historic tram road that bisects a mature cypress and mixed-hardwood swamp.

TOTAL DISTANCE: 10 miles one way.

DIFFICULTY: First 2 miles, easy; upper 8 miles, moderate to difficult.

TIME REQUIRED: Anywhere from an hour to all day, depending on the distance you decide to explore in the swamp.

SPECIAL CONCERNS: Alligators and venomous snakes (mostly cottonmouth moccasins) should be watched for and avoided. Alligators are mostly in the canals adjacent to tram roads and in the interior lakes; cottonmouth moccasins are scattered throughout the preserve. Mosquitoes and biting flies can be bothersome in summer and early fall. Off-trail exploring in the interior of the preserve can be strenuous and often requires wading in knee- to waist-deep water (or deeper). Sunken logs can bruise shins, so jeans are recommended. Carrying a compass (or GPS) and water is highly advised.

SCENIC VALUE: Excellent. This is one of the most picturesque preserves in Florida, although there are those who may find it hard to envision a swamp as being picturesque. Few people get to see the deep and foreboding interior of the swamp, but some of the deep sloughs are fascinating and intriguing. An area dubbed The Cathedral is a deep slough where every available tree branch is literally covered by a bromeliad called the strapleaved guzmania (*Guzmania monostachia*), along with other bromeliads, ferns, peperomias, and orchids. No matter how one feels about swamps, to stand in The Cathedral is one of those memories that will remain with you for a lifetime.

OVERVIEW AND TRAIL DESCRIPTION: The trailhead is located 6.5 miles north of the ranger station on W. J. Janes Memorial Scenic Drive. It is marked by parking areas on both sides of the road and an interpretive sign about the Florida panther. The East Main Trail is an elevated historic tram road that was the principal exit route for the small trains hauling cypress logs out of the swamp for export. The trail entrance is at the north end of the east parking area. Another trail called K-2 is accessible just south of the west parking area where there had once been a private hunting cabin. Part of the K-2 trail is elevated by wood planks across concrete blocks.

Even though the swamp was ravaged for its lumber, it has recovered to the point where it is difficult for anyone to imagine the onslaught that once took place. The swamp appears to be pristine to the casual observer, but the network of tram roads that extend the entire 20-mile length of the swamp and the thousands of cypress stumps scattered throughout the interior attest to the pillage. But all of those cypress stumps have now transformed into prime habitat for ferns and terrestrial orchids and into convenient lounging places for fat cottonmouth moccasins. Another distinctive feature of this swamp is the presence of native royal palms *(Roystonea regia)* that tower well above the other trees. These stately and majestic palms are commonly seen as street trees along roadways of southern and central Florida. It was once thought that the Florida royal palm was a distinct species *(Roystonea elata)*, but recent studies have determined it to be the same species as the Cuban royal palm.

Off-trail exploring is allowed in the preserve, but use your best common sense. A compass is a must and a handheld GPS unit is a bonus. Always remember that Janes Memorial Scenic Drive and the East Main Trail basically run north-south, so if you've hiked east, for instance, into the swamp off of Janes Memorial Scenic Drive, and then wandered north following the deeper drainage sloughs, no matter how far you travel north you can still reach Janes Memorial Scenic Drive by hiking due west, using your trusty compass or GPS. Or you can continue east to arrive at the East Main Trail, presuming you are north of the trailhead. Then head south and you will eventually return to your

vehicle. It is always best to let the park rangers know your travel plans and what time you expect to return. Remember that Janes Memorial Scenic Drive is closed at dusk.

The most famous native orchid in the Fakahatchee Swamp is unquestionably the ghost orchid *(Dendrophylax lindenii; Polyradicion lindenii)*, which flowers from May into August but is typically at its height of bloom season in June and July. The plant has no leaves and is composed only of roots radiating outward from a central point on the mossy trunk or branches of its host tree. A showy white exotic-looking fragrant flower appears at the tip of the flowering stem and seemingly hovers in midair. The flower has been described as looking like an albino frog leaping skyward, and that it does.

The ghost orchid (Polyradicion lindenii), *made famous by the bestselling book* The Orchid Thief, *grows wild only in Collier County, Florida—mostly in the Fakahatchee Strand—and Cuba.*

Globally, the ghost orchid only occurs in Cuba and southern Florida, where it was discovered in 1844 and 1880, respectively.

It was the ghost orchid that inspired Susan Orlean to write her bestseller, *The Orchid Thief*, a true story of a local orchid buff and nurseryman, John Laroche, who was caught and arrested along with Seminole Indians for poaching orchids from the Fakahatchee Strand Preserve State Park. His attorney used the defense that the Seminole Indians who were with him were the ones taking the plants, and as Native Americans they were exempt from state endangered-species laws, even within state and federal parks. Luckily, the judge disagreed, and Laroche and the Seminoles were fined. Later, a fictional movie entitled *Adaptation* was made about the trials and tribulations of Susan Orlean (played by Meryl Streep) trying to produce a movie about her book *The Orchid Thief*.

Guided tours led by park rangers take visitors to sloughs where wild ghost orchids still occur. Even though one must hike into the swamp in the summer when mosquitoes are at their peak, to see a flowering ghost orchid in its native habitat is worth whatever pain and misery you may endure. Ranger-guided walks are offered from November through February on the third Saturday of each month from 10:00 A.M. to noon. Reservations are required. Other guided walks are conducted by volunteers of the Friends of Fakahatchee, which are currently offered beginning at 10:00 A.M. on every first and fourth Tuesday from October through March. A fee is charged for these walks, which goes to benefit the park. For further information about guided tours of the Fakahatchee Strand, phone the park office or visit www.friendsoffakahatchee.org. Guided canoe trips are offered as well.

Big Cypress Bend Boardwalk

TYPE OF TRAIL: Walking.

TYPE OF ADVENTURE: Walk on an elevated boardwalk through a mature cypress and mixed-hardwood swamp.

TOTAL DISTANCE: 0.5 mile.

DIFFICULTY: Easy.

TIME REQUIRED: 1 hour.

SPECIAL CONCERNS: Mosquitoes can be bothersome in summer.

SCENIC VALUE: Excellent. This is a good chance to see the interior of a swamp without getting your feet wet.

OVERVIEW AND TRAIL DESCRIPTION: The trailhead is located 7 miles west of SR 29 on the north side of Tamiami Trail (US 41) at Big Cypress Bend and is marked by signage. This boardwalk extends into the southern terminus of the Faka-

About the Florida Panther

The Florida panther *(Felis concolor coryi)* is a large slender feline that is so rare that it resides on the federal endangered-species list. Other names are puma and cougar. Males weigh up to 160 pounds and females may reach 100 pounds. Both sexes are tawny above and white below and have a long tail with a crook on the end. So-called black panthers are nonexistent, and any reports of these mythical animals can be attributed to Labrador retriever sightings or some other black animal—even young Florida black bears (there are, however, black jaguars in tropical America). Sightings of black Florida panthers rank in the tall-tale category right along with 10-foot and even 20-foot rattlesnakes lurking in Florida's woods. And, by the way, there are Big Foot sightings in the Everglades, too!

The actual number of Florida panthers is probably between fifty and ninety, and highway collisions account for more deaths than from any other source, although habitat destruction is the biggest enemy to all of Florida's wildlife. The Florida panther is currently known to be in four southern Florida counties: Collier, Glades, Hendry, and Miami-Dade, with most of them residing in and around the Fakahatchee Swamp and the Bear Island Unit of the Big Cypress Swamp, both in Collier County. They feed mostly on mammals, and their diet typically includes white-tailed deer, feral hogs, raccoons, opossum, and armadillos.

Most of the wild Florida panthers are collared with radio-telemetry devices to track their movements or to find them should they die, either from natural causes or as a road kill. If a radio-telemetry device does not move for a given amount of time, it sends out a signal. So, drive with caution in panther habitat. And if you should see one of these magnificent animals, consider yourself extremely fortunate.

hatchee Strand. After having read about venomous snakes and other real or perceived dangers that lurk in the Fakahatchee Strand, this is an opportunity for timid visitors to see what a cypress strand looks like from the safety of an elevated boardwalk. Look carefully for birds, reptiles, amphibians, and even mammals, such as raccoons or otters. There is a chance to see white-tailed deer and southern bald eagles, too. An impressive old-growth cypress tree is visible from the boardwalk, and in late spring or early summer, you may get to witness various snakes undergoing their mating ritual. A few native orchids are visible from the boardwalk, so look carefully at the trunks and branches of pond-apple, pop ash, and cypress trees. Even if you are only passing through along Tamiami Trail, this is a nice stop to stretch your legs and enjoy some peace and tranquillity surrounded by nature. And who knows what you might see!

Collier-Seminole State Park

C ollier-Seminole State Park is open 365 days a year from 8:00 A.M. to 7:30 P.M. in summer and from 8:00 A.M. to 5:30 P.M. in winter. The park offers opportunities for camping, canoeing, kayaking, hiking, fishing, photography, wildlife viewing, picnicking, and guided boat tours. Tent and recreational vehicle (RV) camping is available inside the park, and there is a backcountry campsite. Note that alcoholic beverages are prohibited in all Florida state parks.

The park encompasses 6,430 acres with 4,760 acres designated as wilderness areas. Most of the wilderness is mangrove forest, but there are also mixed-hardwood forest, coastal strand, and salt-marsh habitats.

Entrance Fee

$4.00 per vehicle with up to eight passengers; $1.00 for walk-in or bike-in visitors.

Collier-Seminole State Park

TAMIAMI TRAIL

41

92

Marina & Parking ■

COLLIER–SEMINOLE STATE PARK

Blackwater River

Mud Bay

Royal Palm Hammock Creek

River

Blackwater

Palm Bay

Blackwater Bay

N

SCALE 1 : 51,000

0   Kilometers   2

0   Mile   1

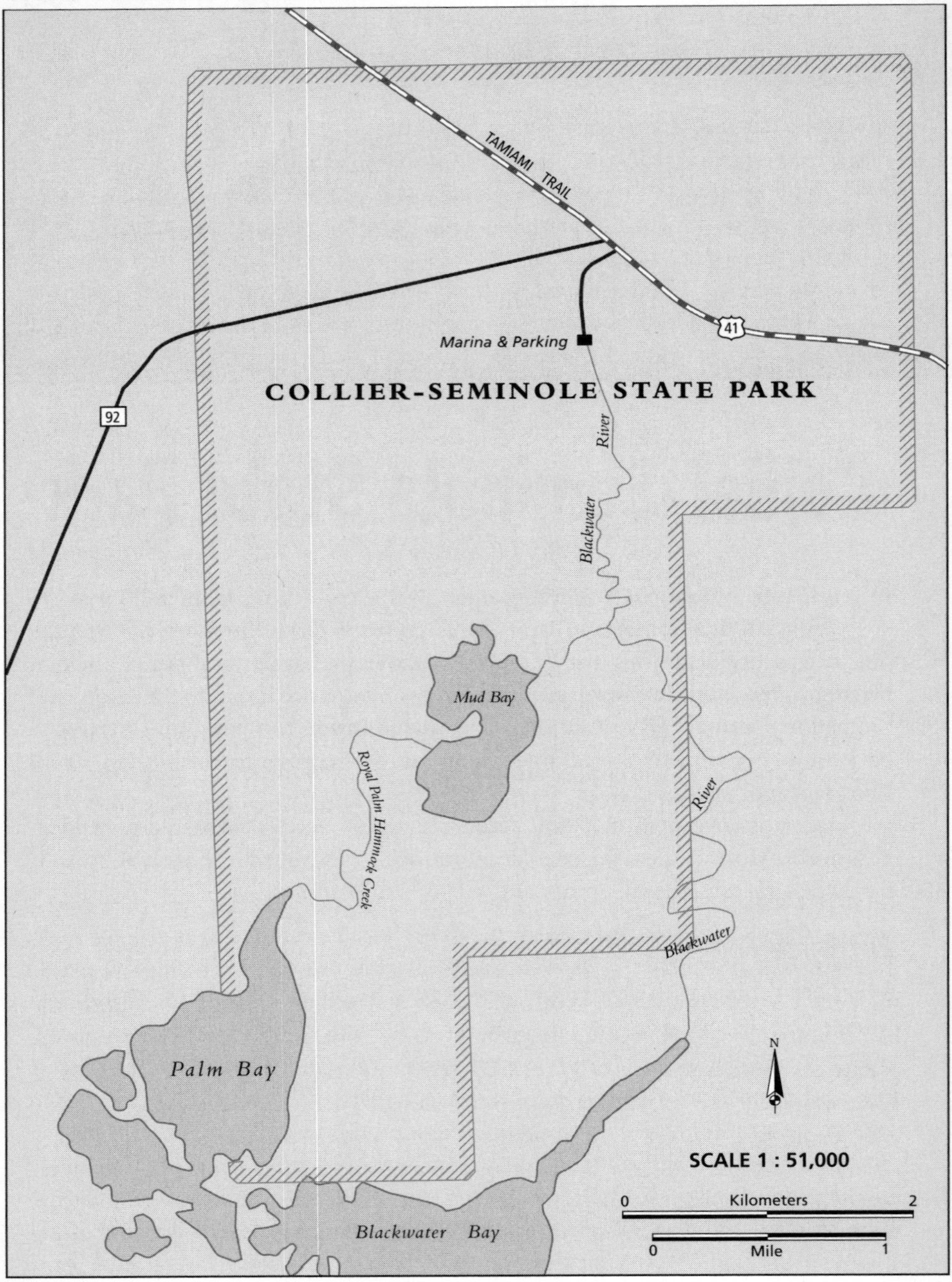

TYPE OF TRAIL: Canoeing or kayaking (powerboats can traverse the Blackwater River portion of the trail).

TYPE OF ADVENTURE: Canoe or kayak through bays and estuarine tidal creeks that traverse mangrove habitat.

TOTAL DISTANCE: 13.5-mile loop.

NAUTICAL CHARTS: NOAA Chart #11430 (Lostmans River to Wiggins Pass) or Waterproof Chart #41 (Everglades & Ten Thousand Islands). There is a free park map available from the ranger station that shows the entire loop as well.

DIFFICULTY: Moderate to strenuous depending on tides and wind conditions.

TIME REQUIRED: All day, so leave early if you plan on completing the entire loop. All canoeists are required to report back to the ranger station by 5:00 P.M. during summer hours, and by 4:00 P.M. during winter hours.

SPECIAL CONCERNS: Mosquitoes and biting flies in summer and fall. Tides can be strong and wind can be a concern in open bays. Check with park rangers for the tide conditions because Mud Bay can be impassable at low tide, especially near the new-moon and full-moon phases. Pets are not allowed in rental canoes. It is not advisable to bring pets along in private canoes either, because dogs attract the attention of large alligators.

SCENIC VALUE: Excellent. There are scenic views along tidal creeks and across open bays with opportunities to view birds, American alligators, American crocodiles, West Indian manatees, bottlenose dolphins, and other wildlife of the region.

OVERVIEW AND TRAIL DESCRIPTION: The trailhead is located inside the park at the surface ramp along the Blackwater River. Be sure to register at the ranger station before you launch. Canoe rentals are available from a concessionaire inside the park, but you must have your own canoe or kayak if you plan to camp in the backcountry. For information regarding canoe rentals and guided boat tours, phone the concessionaire at (239) 642–8898. To make reservations for tent or RV camping inside the park, phone Reserve America toll-free at (800) 326–3521. Reservations cannot be made otherwise.

The Marco Blackwater River Canoe Trail traverses a designated wilderness preserve. In order to maintain its scenic value, there are few markers along the western portions of the trail between Palm Bay and Marker 47 located along

Marco Blackwater River Canoe Trail

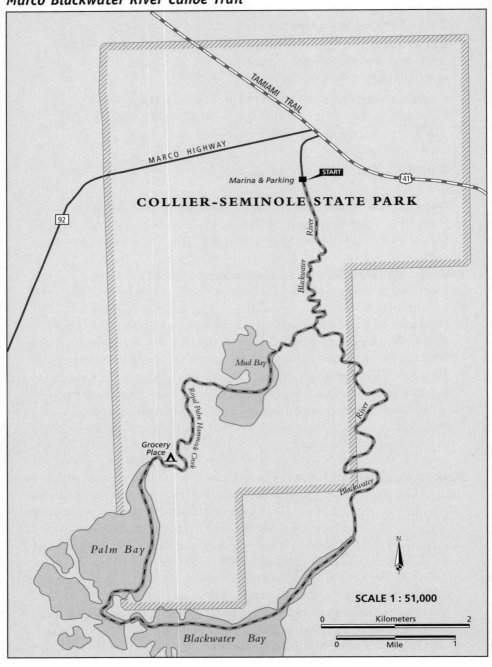

TAMIAMI TRAIL

MARCO HIGHWAY

41

92

Marina & Parking START

COLLIER-SEMINOLE STATE PARK

Blackwater River

Mud Bay

River

Royal Palm Hammock Creek

Grocery Place

Blackwater

Palm Bay

N

Blackwater Bay

SCALE 1 : 51,000

Kilometers
0   2

Mile
0   1

Blackwater River. Be advised that powerboats can access the Blackwater River from either inside the park or from areas outside the park. Primitive tent camping is available at the Grocery Place campsite located between Palm Bay and Mud Bay. To access this campsite from the Blackwater River without completing the entire loop, turn right into the creek at Marker 47, assuming the tide is high enough to allow passage across Mud Bay.

There are ample fishing opportunities in this area, and fish to target are spotted seatrout, snook, redfish, gray (mangrove) snapper, black drum, and sheepshead. Be sure to check on license requirements as well as fishing regulations and restrictions before wetting a line.

Now-extinct Calusa Indians once inhabited this region. When you are paddling along the rivers and creeks, you are exploring the same areas they traversed in dugout canoes more than 300 years ago. Calusa Indians were hunter-fisher-gatherers, living close to the sea as did their counterparts, the Tequesta Indians, along Florida's southeast coast. These indigenous people hunted land animals along with American alligators, American crocodiles, fish (including sharks), sea turtles, West Indian manatees, West Indian monk seals (now extinct), mollusks, and other marine life. It was the Calusa Indians who mortally wounded Juan Ponce de Leon during his second voyage in 1521 to the land he called *La Florida*. He died in Cuba and is buried in Puerto Rico, where he was once governor.

Although modern writers often glamorize these early explorers, most were ruthless conquerors who wanted nothing more than to take slaves and plunder the natural resources. Ponce de Leon was no exception. So during your journey along the Blackwater River and its tributaries, imagine how much more difficult it would be in a heavy dugout canoe with crude paddles. Perhaps then your own personal experience in your modern-day canoe or kayak will not seem so arduous!

Collier-Seminole Nature Trail

TYPE OF TRAIL: Walking.

TYPE OF ADVENTURE: Walk along a loop trail to an elevated boardwalk and observation deck over freshwater marsh habitat.

TOTAL DISTANCE: 0.9 mile round-trip.

DIFFICULTY: Easy.

TIME REQUIRED: Half an hour or more.

SPECIAL CONCERNS: Mosquitoes and biting flies in summer and fall.

SCENIC VALUE: Excellent. The boardwalk terminates at an elevated deck with a scenic view of marsh vegetation and associated birds and other wildlife.

Freshwater marshes in the wet season are interesting habitats to explore if you don't mind getting your feet wet. Wading birds can be abundant.

OVERVIEW AND TRAIL DESCRIPTION: Turn left at the first turnoff past the park entrance. The trailhead is located on the north side of the parking lot at the end of this turnoff. The trail has a loop in the middle with interpretive signs along the way to help identify native plants and other natural features that can be viewed from the trail. The park brochure advertises this as a great trail for families with children. Bring binoculars and a camera.

Collier-Seminole Hiking and Biking Trail

TYPE OF TRAIL: Hiking or biking.

TYPE OF ADVENTURE: Hike or bike along an elevated loop trail through freshwater marsh habitat.

TOTAL DISTANCE: 3.5 miles round-trip.

DIFFICULTY: Easy to moderate.

TIME REQUIRED: Allow for 2 hours on foot and 1 hour on a bike.

SPECIAL CONCERNS: Mosquitoes and biting flies in summer and fall.

SCENIC VALUE: Excellent. This is a nice sandy trail to walk or bike while viewing birds and other wildlife, as well as native flowering plants.

OVERVIEW AND TRAIL DESCRIPTION: The trailhead is located north of the park entrance along Tamiami Trail (U.S. Highway 41) and is indicated by a parking area and signage. This is a loop trail and is advertised by the park as a great trail for bikes and avid walkers. A portion of this trail was once the original road that early settlers used to access Marco Island, prior to the completion of Tamiami Trail in 1928. This is an excellent trail for spending some time, so hike or bike slowly so you won't miss anything. There is a pond located along the trail where you may get the opportunity to see birds, alligators, turtles, snakes, frogs, and other resident wildlife.

Collier-Seminole Wilderness Adventure Trail

TYPE OF TRAIL: Hiking.

TYPE OF ADVENTURE: Hike along a designated trail through mixed-hardwood swamp, cypress strand, and other scenic habitats with the option to camp at a primitive campsite.

TOTAL DISTANCE: 7 miles to complete the longer loop, but a shorter 3-mile loop is also available from the same trailhead.

DIFFICULTY: Moderate to strenuous.

TIME REQUIRED: 3 hours or more.

SPECIAL CONCERNS: Mosquitoes and biting flies in summer and fall. Muddy or flooded with shallow water during the rainy season, so wear shoes you don't mind getting wet. No potable water or facilities along the trail.

SCENIC VALUE: Excellent. A portion of this trail leads through a mixed-hardwood swamp with native royal palms towering above the forest.

OVERVIEW AND TRAIL DESCRIPTION: The trailhead is located south of the park entrance on the west side of Tamiami Trail (US 41). If you just want to hike the 3-mile loop, do not turn on either of the trails leading north. Taking the first left turn to the north will lead you along the longer 7-mile loop trail. If you have the time and willingness to explore this region, this can be a very rewarding trail. Orange markings on the trees help designate the trail for hikers. Florida panthers, Florida black bears, bobcats, deer, and other mammals inhabit this region, so if you find any muddy areas look for their tracks. If you're lucky you might even get to see the animal that made the tracks!

There are lots of opportunities for bird-watching, and even butterfly and dragonfly watching, so stop periodically to assess your surroundings. Look for birds of prey, including bald eagles, swallow-tailed kites, and ospreys, soaring overhead. Some of the trees are festooned with epiphytic plants, such as bromeliads, ferns, orchids, and mosses, so take the time to observe not only the trees but also what's growing on them. Open sunny areas can be very rewarding if you want to see unusual wildflowers of the region.

It is always advisable to let the rangers know you are planning to hike the 7-mile loop trail so if, for some unexpected reason, you do not return on time they will know of your approximate whereabouts. If you feel like you are lost, a due west heading will eventually lead you to Tamiami Trail. You did remember to bring a compass, didn't you?

If you plan on camping, you are required to notify the ranger station in person. Be sure to pick up the free handout for the Collier-Seminole State Park hiking trails while you are at the station. The backpacker's campsite is located at the terminus of a short side trail that leads west into the interior of the loop. The shortest route is to continue straight past the first left turn from the trailhead and then take the second left (north) turn. This part of the trail will lead north and then west. The campsite trail turns to the west once the trail begins its turn back to the north. The longer route for more adventurous hikers is to take the first left and when this northerly portion of the trail turns back to the south, the backpacker's campsite trail will turn to the right (west) before the main trail turns to the east. There are no facilities—you are required to bring your own food, water, and gear. Cook stoves are recommended for cooking, and campers are advised to secure their food at night from raccoons or possibly even black bears (a rarity, but you never know). Out of courtesy to other campers, always bury human waste and any decomposable food scraps away from the campsite. Pets, horses, bicycles, off-road vehicles, and weapons are prohibited. Campfires are allowed in designated sites.

Corkscrew Swamp Sanctuary

C orkscrew Swamp is the premier National Audubon Society sanctuary in the United States. This is a definite destination if you have an interest in Florida's flora and fauna—especially birds. And the good news is that you can quietly explore more than 2 miles of swamp on an elevated boardwalk! The boardwalk begins and ends at the Blair Audubon Center where visitors can receive firsthand information about the sanctuary from very informative volunteers and Audubon employees at the front desk. Inside the Blair Audubon Center is The Nature Store, which offers an impressive array of books, videos, clothing, binoculars, cameras and equipment, bird feeders, birdhouses, jewelry, an assortment of games and toys for children of all ages, and much more. There are even soothing music CDs along with recordings of Florida bird-songs for your listening and learning enjoyment.

Also located inside the Blair Audubon Center are the Swamp Senses Media Theater, restrooms, classrooms, a photo gallery, and a food service that offers cold sandwiches, drinks, and snacks that can either be eaten there or enjoyed outdoors in the front picnic area. Along the back of the Blair Audubon Center is a covered porch with benches and comfortable rocking chairs to relax in, and these are perfect locations to watch the bird feeders. These feeders attract such

Corkscrew Swamp Sanctuary

Cape Coral

Fort Myers

82

Southwest Florida
International Airport

L E E

29

850 CORKSCREW ROAD

CREW Marsh

*Estero
Bay*

Estero

*Corkscrew
Swamp
Sanctuary*

*Lake
Trafford*

Immokalee

41

846

29

Bonita Springs

858

IMMOKALEE ROAD 846

ALLIGATOR ALLEY

I–75

COLLIER

Naples

951

839

GULF OF MEXICO

TAMIAMI TRAIL

29

41

**MARCO
ISLAND**

*Gullivan
Bay*

Ochopee

SCALE 1 : 576,000

0   Kilometers   20

0   Miles   20

N

Chokoloskee

birds as painted buntings, indigo buntings, sparrows, woodpeckers, cardinals, blue jays, and other resident and seasonal species, viewable right from your rocking chair! The sanctuary is also prime habitat for Florida panthers, Florida black bears, white-tailed deer, and other wildlife. This is wild Florida without a theme park, so don't miss it!

Admission

Adults: $10.00; full-time college students with identification: $6.00; members of National Audubon Society with membership card: $5.00; students age six through eighteen: $4.00; children younger than age six admitted free.

National Audubon Society Membership

To receive a National Audubon Society member discount to enter Corkscrew Swamp Sanctuary, you can join the society for $20 per year, which includes membership in your state and local chapters along with receiving *Audubon* magazine each month. To become a member, inquire in the Blair Audubon Center at Corkscrew Swamp Sanctuary, visit National Audubon Society's Web site at www.audubon.org, or write to Audubon, Membership Data Center, P.O. Box 51003, Boulder, CO 80323.

Corkscrew Swamp Sanctuary Boardwalk

TYPE OF TRAIL: Walking. Wheelchair accessible.

TYPE OF ADVENTURE: Walk along an elevated boardwalk and view an abundance of birdlife, along with other wildlife, in their natural habitat.

TOTAL DISTANCE: 2.25-mile loop or a shorter 1-mile loop.

DIFFICULTY: Easy.

TIME REQUIRED: 3 hours or more to fully enjoy what the swamp has to offer.

SPECIAL CONCERNS: Mosquitoes never seem to be very bothersome because of the slow-moving water and an abundance of mosquitofish (*Gambusia*) that eat them in their larval stage.

SCENIC VALUE: Outstanding. This elevated boardwalk offers extraordinary scenic views of what wild Florida looked like before much of it was lost to development and agriculture.

OVERVIEW AND TRAIL DESCRIPTION: The trailhead begins directly outside of the Blair Audubon Center with an elevated boardwalk that leads visitors through pine flatwoods, cypress and mixed-hardwood swamp, wet prairies, and pond-apple sloughs that make up the 11,000-acre preserve. The entire boardwalk is more than 2 miles in length, and there are covered pavilions and sitting areas along the way to either relax or escape getting caught in a rainstorm. There is a shorter 1-mile loop that allows for a shorter excursion.

Corkscrew Swamp is extraordinarily wild and beautiful, but it is the birdlife that attracts thousands of visitors to this special place each year. A great variety of birds are visible from the boardwalk, and the surrounding swamp is a major wood stork rookery. The best times to see wood stork nesting activities are late winter and early spring. Dedicated and informed volunteers are often stationed along the boardwalk in strategic locations to help point out some of the hidden secrets that the casual visitor might not see. Barred owls are often visible in daytime, and volunteers may have spotting scopes trained on them for visitors to

The ubiquitous native butterfly orchid (Encyclia tampensis) *is the most common epiphytic orchid in Florida. It blooms in summertime.*

stop and take a closer look. There is much to see, so this is definitely not a place for a hurried visit. Seasoned and amateur bird watchers alike will find this to be one of the most rewarding and memorable places to visit in Florida.

Some of Florida's prettiest, rarest, and most interesting native plants can be seen from the boardwalk too, including flowering native orchids such as the butterfly orchid *(Encyclia tampensis)*, the clamshell orchid *(Prosthechea cochleata)*, and the exotic blossoms of the night-scented orchid *(Epidendrum nocturnum)* that emits a strong odor at night to attract sphinx moth pollinators. The showy and scented white blossoms of the string-lily *(Crinum americanum)* brighten the wet prairies and edges of sloughs. Deeper areas will harbor pickerelweed *(Pontederia cordata)*, with spikes of butterfly-attracting blue flowers, and at least two species of arrowhead *(Sagittaria lancifolia* and *Sagittaria graminea)*, both with three-petaled white flowers. Bromeliads abound in the trees and the most common species, the cardinal airplant or stiff-leaved wild-pine *(Tillandsia fasciculata)*, forms large clusters of urnlike plants with branched spikes of showy red-and-yellow bracts. If you're lucky, you might get to see ruby-throated hummingbirds sipping nectar from the tubular purple flowers that are almost hidden by the bracts.

Corkscrew Swamp Sanctuary is one of the real gems of Florida. Walk slowly, stop often, and listen attentively for the sounds of nature, like the loud calls and hammering of pileated woodpeckers, the croaking of countless frogs, or even the eerie and plaintive calls of the limpkin. An array of colorful songbirds can be seen, especially during fall and spring migration when warblers are present in vast numbers.

Corkscrew Regional Ecosystem Watershed (CREW Marsh)

The CREW Land and Water Trust manages 5,000 acres of pine flatwoods, mesic hammocks, and freshwater marsh in southwest Florida. This is a portion of a 60,000-acre land-acquisition project. Relatively few people know of this preserve, much less enjoy the 5 miles of trails available to hikers. This is surprising because the site is contiguous with Corkscrew Swamp Sanctuary, which welcomes thousands of visitors yearly. The hiking trails at CREW Marsh are well maintained but some portions of the trails may be flooded during the rainy season. The trails are closed to hikers when resource managers conduct prescribed burns or when there are wildfires.

Location

From Tamiami Trail (U.S. Highway 41) turn north onto State Road 29 and proceed north through the city of Immokalee. About 5 miles past the city limits, turn left (west) onto State Road 82. Drive west a few miles to County Road

Corkscrew Regional Ecosystem Watershed (CREW Marsh)

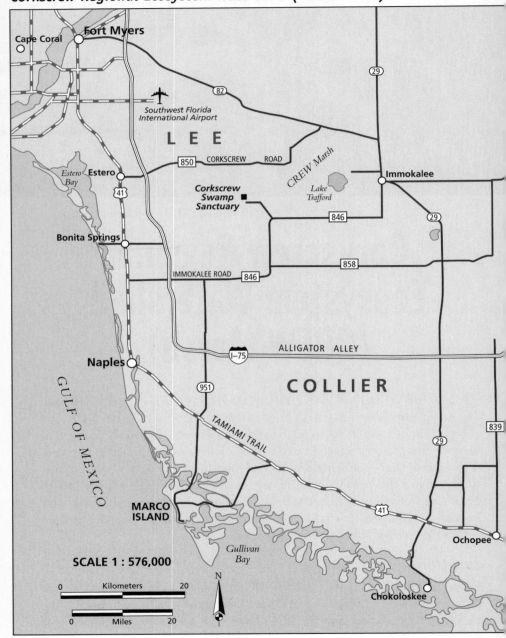

850 (Corkscrew Road) and turn left (south). The main entrance is 1.5 miles far-ther on your left, with the entrance sign on a wood fence with bold blue letters.

From Interstate 75 take exit 123 and turn left (east) onto Corkscrew Road (CR 850). Proceed about 18 miles and the entrance is on your right (keep going past the locked gate entrances until you arrive at the main entrance).

Guided Hikes

Naturalist-guided walks are conducted free of charge (although donations are gladly accepted) on the second Saturday of each month from November through April beginning at 9:00 A.M. There are also guided walks offered on every Thursday at 9:00 A.M. from November through March. For even more adventure there are guided night hikes ($5.00 per person; children younger than age six admitted free) during the winter months. Preregistration is required for special guided night hikes.

Guided hikes are a great way to learn from very knowledgeable employees and volunteers about the local flora and fauna, as well as the history of the pre-serve. Another way to enjoy a guided walk at the CREW Marsh is by joining in on the festivities associated with the annual Wildflower Weekend held at the site in either March or April. Guides take groups around a loop trail and point out, identify, and offer interesting information about the varied and abundant wildflowers visible along the trail. One rather special wildflower, the grass-pink orchid *(Calopogon tuberosus)* is usually in flower for this event. Slide presenta-tions featuring local wildflowers are offered the Friday evening prior to the event. For further information on trail accessibility, guided walks, and Wild-flower Weekend, or to schedule group tours, contact the CREW Land and Water Trust at (239) 657–2253 or e-mail crewtrust@earthlink.net. Whether you are on a guided walk or enjoying a quiet and peaceful walk alone or with friends, be sure to bring your binoculars and camera.

Camping

There is primitive camping available at the CREW Marsh for individuals and groups. The campsite is available by special permit and can accommodate up to twenty campers. From the main parking lot at the trailhead, there is a 2-mile hike to a campsite where you will find a picnic table and grill available. Be advised that campfires are not allowed except by special permission, and even then there must be favorable weather conditions (no dry-season fires). To inquire about the availability of the campsite, or to obtain a permit, phone the CREW Land and Water Trust. If the campsite is available, they will either mail or fax a form to you that must be filled out and returned. You will then receive a permit along with a map to the campsite. Dogs are allowed but they must be kept on a leash at all times.

Trails

There is a printable self-guided tour brochure available on the CREW Land and Water Trust Web site (www.crewtrust.org). It has a small map of the trails and interpretation that coincides with numbered posts along the Pine Flatwoods Loop Trail and the Marsh Loop Trail. Brochures are also at the kiosk near the trailhead. There are a number of loop trails available that traverse habitats ranging from freshwater marsh, pine flatwoods, mesic hammock, and pop ash slough, and these trails can be very interesting at all seasons. The site includes the Pine Flatwoods Loop Trail, Hammock Trail, Pop Ash Swamp Trail, Marsh Loop Trail, and an alternative marsh trail. All of the trails eventually connect to one another, so it's easy to pick and choose the distance you wish to travel.

Miami-Dade County Parks and Preserves

I f you are an urban explorer, there are some fine parks and preserves worth visiting in the Metropolitan Miami area. The Miami-Dade Parks Department manages more than 10,000 acres of natural areas, which contain remnants of habitats once associated with the historical Everglades that covered all of southern Florida. These habitats include tropical hardwood hammocks, pine rocklands, mangroves, coastal strand, beach dunes, freshwater marsh, and salt marsh. And some county parks are among the best bird-watching sites in South Florida. Following are two of the best parks for nature lovers to visit. Additional nature-oriented Miami-Dade County parks and preserves are listed in the Appendix, or visit www.miamidade.gov/parks.

Miami-Dade County Parks and Preserves

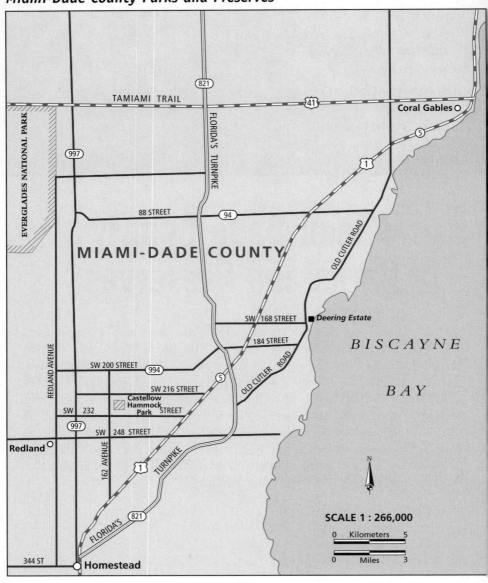

TAMIAMI TRAIL

EVERGLADES NATIONAL PARK

FLORIDA'S TURNPIKE

821

41

Coral Gables ○

5

997

1

88 STREET

94

OLD CUTLER ROAD

MIAMI-DADE COUNTY

SW 168 STREET ■ Deering Estate

184 STREET

BISCAYNE

REDLAND AVENUE

SW 200 STREET

994

OLD CUTLER ROAD

BAY

SW 216 STREET

5

Castellow
Hammock
Park STREET

SW 232

997

SW 248 STREET

Redland ○

162 AVENUE

1

TURNPIKE

N

FLORIDA'S

821

SCALE 1 : 266,000

0   Kilometers   5

344 ST

Homestead ○

0   Miles   3

Castellow Hammock Park

TYPE OF TRAIL: Hiking.

TYPE OF ADVENTURE: Hike on a self-guided trail through a mature tropical hardwood hammock.

TOTAL DISTANCE: 0.75-mile round-trip.

DIFFICULTY: Easy to moderate.

TIME REQUIRED: 1 hour.

SPECIAL CONCERNS: Some exposed limestone and tree roots. Moderate mosquitoes in summer.

SCENIC VALUE: Excellent.

OVERVIEW AND TRAIL DESCRIPTION: The trailhead begins on the east side of the nature center and is marked by signage. Numbered posts correspond to a trail-guide booklet available at the nature center, and there are lists of birds, butterflies, reptiles and amphibians, and plants that occur within the park. Castellow Hammock once boasted the tallest tree canopy of any hammock in South Florida and the forest harbored three national champion trees. Following Hurricane Andrew in 1992, about 85 percent of the mature trees in the hammock were toppled. Many of the felled trees are visible from the nature trail, including the previous national champion wild tamarind *(Lysiloma latisiliquum)*. This grand tree once stood 115 feet tall with a trunk circumference of 8½ feet at breast height. The hammock has since recovered with a much lower canopy, although the national champion false mastic *(Sideroxylon foetidissimum)* still towers well above 100 feet tall.

The park is a renowned bird-watching destination for people who travel from around the world to see painted buntings that frequent the park's feeders from October into May each year. Male painted buntings have bright blue heads with a red eye ring, a green back, and red undersides. They are unquestionably one of the most brilliantly colored birds in America. Other sought-after birds at the park include indigo buntings, western kingbirds, scissor-tailed flycatchers, black-whiskered vireos, bronzed cowbirds, summer tanagers, Swainson's hawks, and practically every species of migrating warbler that passes through southern Florida. The park's bird list includes more than 130 species.

An educational hummingbird and butterfly garden next to the nature center attracts ruby-throated hummingbirds and rufous hummingbirds to the abundance of flowers from fall into spring. Butterflies abound and some of the unusual species include the dina yellow, dingy purplewing, and malachite. To date the park's butterfly list includes sixty-nine species. Recent reports of rare and unusual bird and butterfly sightings in South Florida are posted on an out-

Castellow Hammock Park

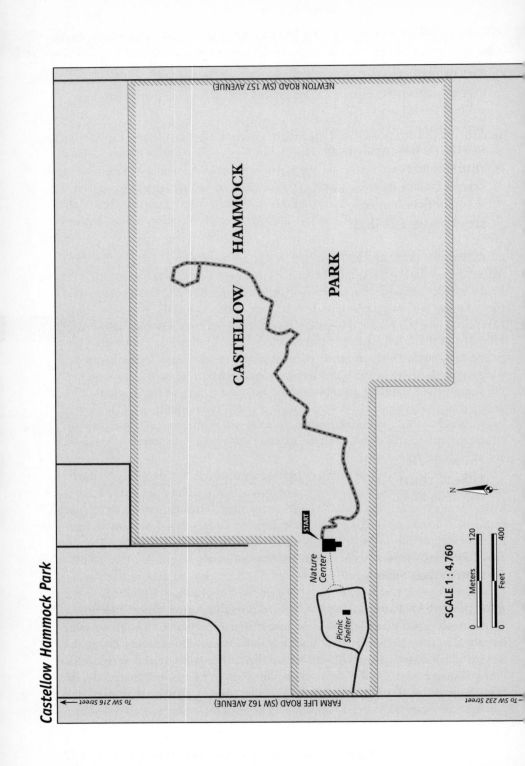

NEWTON ROAD (SW 157 AVENUE)

CASTELLOW HAMMOCK

PARK

START

Nature
Center

Picnic
Shelter

N

SCALE 1 : 4,760

Meters   0   120

Feet   0   400

To SW 216 Street

FARM LIFE ROAD (SW 162 AVENUE)

To SW 232 Street

door bulletin board, and the postings are updated frequently. The Miami Blue Chapter of the North American Butterfly Association holds their quarterly meetings in the nature center, and these educational meetings are open to the public.

The park's normal hours of operation are 8:00 A.M. to 4:30 P.M. daily but walk-in visitors are welcome from dawn to dusk. Castellow Hammock Park naturalists offer professional and informative guided walks, bike hikes, canoe trips, and van trips throughout South Florida, including Everglades National Park, Big Cypress National Preserve, the Florida Keys, and other wilderness areas. Upcoming field trips, classes, and special events offered by park staff, as well as field trips conducted by Tropical Audubon Society and local chapters of the North American Butterfly Association, are posted on an outdoor bulletin board.

Inside the nature center are displays on tree snails, South Florida archaeology, and historical aspects of the region. There is also a covered picnic shelter, so be sure to bring lunch or a snack to enjoy in this peaceful setting.

Deering Estate at Cutler

TYPE OF TRAIL: Hiking or motorized tram. Wheelchair accessible.

TYPE OF ADVENTURE: Hike or ride on a motorized tram along a historic trail through Addison Hammock to a Tequesta Indian burial mound; join park naturalists on a guided tour of Charles Deering's stone mansion and the historic Richmond Cottage; walk along an elevated boardwalk through coastal mangroves; enjoy one of the most stunning views of Biscayne Bay.

TOTAL DISTANCE: The main trail through Addison Hammock is about 1 mile round-trip; the mangrove boardwalk is 0.5 mile round-trip.

DIFFICULTY: Easy.

TIME REQUIRED: 1 hour to hike the main trail with a guide.

SPECIAL CONCERNS: Mosquitoes in summer and fall.

SCENIC VALUE: Superb.

OVERVIEW AND TRAIL DESCRIPTION: The entrance fee into the park ($7.00 adults; $5.00 children age four through fourteen; children age three years or younger admitted free) includes a guided hike or tram ride through Addison Hammock as well as a guided tour of the historic buildings. The main trail through Addison Hammock is only available to the public when accompanied by a guide, but the mangrove boardwalk can be enjoyed on your own. The main trail represents a historic road that was hand-cleared all the way to Coconut Grove as a trade route to carry goods to market.

The Deering Estate at Cutler has a rich history. The Cutler Fossil Site on the property is where archaeologists uncovered bones of many interesting now-extinct animals, including dire wolves, saber-tooth cats, short-faced bears, American lions, mastodons, mammoths, California condors, and a host of other creatures. The remains of Paleo-Indians that date from 10,000 years ago were also unearthed at the site. An extensive Tequesta Indian midden and burial sites exist here as well, offering an opportunity to learn about these now-extinct early inhabitants of southeastern Florida. Due to freshwater springs close to Biscayne Bay, this site became a popular stopping place for early explorers and settlers. It was part of a larger area that the Seminoles called the Hunting Grounds because of the wealth of flora and fauna that could be harvested from the region.

Settlers made their homes here as well—the most famous being Charles Deering (1852–1927), a wealthy industrialist who built his stone mansion at the site in the 1920s, surrounded by more than 400 acres of hammock, pine rock-land, mangroves, and salt marsh. The view from Deering's mansion is breathtaking. The site was destined to become yet another enclave for the wealthy when it was targeted by developers in the 1980s who were proposing to build lavish and expensive bayfront homes on the property. Public outcry and pressure from environmental groups prompted the Miami-Dade County Commission and the State of Florida to purchase the property as a public treasure. The buildings were restored after Hurricane Andrew ravaged them in 1992 with winds in excess of 165 mph along with a 17-foot storm surge that swept across the property.

Today the Deering Estate at Cutler welcomes visitors from around the world who wish to learn more about the rich history and abundant resources of the park. In addition to guided hikes and historic-building tours, park natural-ists offer canoe trips to Chicken Key, a small island located about 1 mile off-shore in Biscayne Bay, as well as special bird and butterfly walks on the second and third Saturdays each month, respectively. You can bring your own canoe or kayak and launch at the People's Dock, which has been recently restored and now offers public access to Biscayne Bay. Efforts are currently under way to offer canoe and kayak rentals at the park as well. Besides the mangrove shore-line, there are some interesting creeks along the edge of Biscayne Bay that are worth exploring, and there are opportunities to fish and even take a refreshing dip in the bay. Strong winds can make canoeing in Biscayne Bay a challenge, but tidal currents are not a problem on this side of the bay. Bird-watching along the edge of the bay can be exceptional, especially at low tide. Watch for herons, egrets, shorebirds, magnificent frigatebirds, pelicans, roseate spoonbills,

About Biscayne Bay

Juan Ponce de Leon wrote in 1513 of finding a "bright nameless great bay and fresh springs" during his travels around the land that he called *La Florida*. He called it *Chequescha*, which is almost certainly a word used for the bay by the indigenous people who lived along its shores. These people would later be called the Tequesta Indians by Spanish explorers. And in 1566 Pedro Menendez de Aviles, founder of St. Augustine and the appointed governor of Florida, sailed into this bay for water from the same "fresh springs" noted by Ponce de Leon.

The origin of the modern name of the bay is open to conjecture. One source says it was named after the Bay of Biscay, which borders France and Spain. But Hernando Fontaneda wrote in 1575 of finding a wrecked ship in the bay that was owned by *El Biscaino,* a man from the Spanish province of Biscaya. A map of 1765 shows the name *Vizcaino*. On a map dated 1837, it was called Sandwich Gulf, presumably because it was sandwiched in between the Florida mainland and the sand barrier island of Key Biscayne as well as the rocky Upper Florida Keys.

Today Biscayne Bay is a focal point and source of recreation for local residents and more than 10 million tourists who travel to the Greater Miami area each year. But greedy developers and politicians once threatened this crown jewel. The proposed city of Islandia was to encompass the island of Elliott Key (now in Biscayne National Park) and other keys that border Biscayne Bay and the Straits of Florida in the Upper Florida Keys. A causeway from Key Biscayne was to allow access to beachfront resorts and multimillion dollar homes. An even more grandiose plan was to dredge the southern bay into a deepwater port so tankers and cruise ships could gain access to the bay via deep channels dredged through offshore reefs. Luckily for the people of Florida, and for the flora and fauna of Biscayne Bay itself, none of these visions made it past the planning stages. Much of the bay is now protected within Biscayne National Park, the first national park that is mostly underwater. Whether you are a sailor, water-sports enthusiast, angler, or simply someone who likes to sit and meditate along the shores of Biscayne Bay, the result is still the same—pure pleasure.

ospreys, mangrove cuckoos, white-crowned pigeons, and the occasional bald eagle or peregrine falcon. American crocodiles, West Indian manatees, bottlenose dolphins, and even river otters can sometimes be seen close to shore. Adding to the natural beauty of the mangrove shoreline along Biscayne Bay is the skyline of Greater Miami and Key Biscayne, complete with lavish homes bordering the bay—a reminder that you are exploring next to a major metropolitan area.

National Parks and Preserves

www.nps.gov/parks
All visitor centers are wheelchair accessible.

Biscayne National Park
9700 Southwest 328 Street
Homestead, FL 33033
Convoy Point Visitor Center: (305) 230–7275

Everglades National Park
40001 State Road 9336
Homestead, FL 33034
Main office: (305) 242–7700
Ernest F. Coe Visitor Center: (305) 242–7700
Royal Palm Visitor Center: (305) 242–7700 (Coe Visitor Center receptionist)
Flamingo Visitor Center: (239) 695–2945 (staffed intermittently in summer)
Shark Valley Visitor Center: (305) 221–8776
Gulf Coast Visitor Center: (239) 695–3311
Twenty-four-hour Emergency Dispatch: (305) 242–7740

Big Cypress National Preserve
HCR 61, Box 110
Ochopee, FL 33943
Big Cypress Visitor Center at Oasis: (239) 695–1201
www.nps.gov/bicy

Useful Web Sites

www.FLAUSA.com
This is the State of Florida's official travel-planning Web site.

www.myflorida.com
This is the official portal of the State of Florida.

Florida State Parks and Preserves

Web site: www.floridastateparks.org
Some of the Florida state parks listed below are not covered in this guide but are listed here because they do have areas worth exploring. For further information please contact the individual parks.

Bill Baggs Cape Florida State Park
1200 South Crandon Boulevard
Key Biscayne, FL 33149
Park office: (305) 361–5811

Collier-Seminole State Park
20200 Tamiami Trail South
Naples, FL 33114
Park office: (239) 394–3397

Fakahatchee Strand Preserve State Park
P.O. Box 548
Copeland, FL 33926
Park office: (239) 695–4593

Oleta River State Park
3400 Northeast 163 Street
North Miami, FL 33160
Park office: (305) 919–1846

The Barnacle Historic State Park
3485 Main Highway
Coconut Grove, FL 33133
Park office: (305) 442–6866

Miami-Dade County Parks and Preserves

E-mail: parks@miamidade.gov
www.miamidade.gov/parks
Department office: (305) 755–7800

The following Miami-Dade County parks either encompass natural areas that are worth exploring or are coastal parks with access to Biscayne Bay. Visit the Web site for scheduled naturalist-guided field trips, classes, and special events. An Eco-Adventure Newsletter is available by phoning (305)

365–3018 at Crandon Park. This free quarterly newsletter covers all nature-oriented programs and field trips offered through the Miami-Dade Parks and Recreation Department. Eco-Adventure tours (biking, hiking, canoeing, kayaking) are also available for conventions, conferences, and other large groups.

A. D. "Doug" Barnes Park
3401 Southwest 72 Avenue
Miami, FL 33155
Park office: (305) 666–5883
Nature Center: (305) 662–4124

Bill Sadowski Park
17555 Southwest 79 Avenue
Palmetto Bay, FL 33157
Park office: (305) 255–4767

Black Point Park & Marina
24775 Southwest 87 Avenue
Miami, FL 33032
Park office: (305) 258–4092

Camp Owaissa Bauer
17001 Southwest 264 Street
Redland, FL 33031
Park office: (305) 247–6016

Castellow Hammock Park
22301 Southwest 162 Avenue
Redland, FL 33170
Park office: (305) 242–7688

Crandon Park & Marina
4000 Crandon Boulevard
Key Biscayne, FL 33149
Park office: (305) 361–5421
Eco-Adventure and Eco-Tours office: (305) 365–3018 (countywide)

Deering Estate at Cutler
16701 Southwest 72 Avenue
Palmetto Bay, FL 33157
Park office: (305) 235–1668

Greynolds Park
17530 West Dixie Highway
Miami, FL 33160
Park office: (305) 945–3425

Haulover Park & Marina
10800 Collins Avenue
Miami Beach, FL 33139
Park office: (305) 944–3040

Homestead Bayfront Park and Marina
9698 Southwest 328 Street
Homestead, FL 33033
Park office: (305) 230-3033

Larry and Penny Thompson Park
12451 Southwest 184 Street
Miami, FL 33177
Park office and campground: (305) 232–1049

Matheson Hammock Park & Marina
9610 Old Cutler Road
Coral Gables, FL 33156
Park office: (305) 665–5475

National Audubon Society

Corkscrew Swamp Sanctuary
375 Sanctuary Road West
Naples, FL 34120
Blair Audubon Center: (239) 348–9151

South Florida Water Management District— Corkscrew Regional Watershed (CREW)

CREW MARSH (CREW Land & Water Trust)
23998 Corkscrew Road
Estero, FL 33928
Main office: (239) 657–2253
www.crewtrust.org

Appendix B
Canoe Safety Tips

- Although all canoeists (and kayakers) are required by state law to carry a whistle on board, it is advisable to also bring along a flare gun and/or an aerosol air horn in case of emergencies. (These are *required* if your canoe is motorized, plus you must have the registration numbers and decal properly displayed on the bow of a motorized canoe and have your registration on board; motorized canoes can be registered at any auto tag agency.) Also consider bringing either a cell phone or a handheld VHF marine radio (sealed in a waterproof container). Cell phones sometimes work if you are relatively close to either Flamingo or Everglades City, but most will not work in remote areas of the Everglades. The twenty-four-hour dispatch phone number for Everglades National Park is (305) 242–7740. If it is a nonemergency and you have a VHF marine radio, you can try to contact patrolling park rangers or fishermen with VHF marine radios on board their vessel. Use Channel 16. Satellite phones are another option.

- Emergency Situations: If you are in a life-threatening situation or have a medical emergency, send a maritime distress and safety call to facilitate search and rescue. Many marine radios are equipped with a distress key that, when pressed, automatically sends a distress signal along with the latitude and longitude of the vessel. Handheld radios usually need to be connected to a GPS (Global Positioning System) unit in order to send latitude and longitude positions. When the distress signal is activated, the radio will "shadow watch" for a transmission between Channel 16 and Channel 70 until an acknowledgment signal is received. If no acknowledgment is received, the distress call is repeated every few seconds. When a distress acknowledgment is received, a distress alarm sounds and Channel 16 is automatically selected so you can give specific details of your situation to your contact. The signal range may vary, but under normal conditions the range should be approximately 20 nautical miles. *Always remain with your vessel near a navigational marker or campsite and try to hail another boater.* A red flag or three blasts on an air horn or whistle are international distress signals.

- If you have a handheld GPS, bring it along. Some GPS units have map capabilities that augment the information already on base maps. Regional maps can be downloaded into the GPS unit from computer software (CD-ROM), or some units may even allow the use of computerized map cards (there is one available for the Everglades). With these maps you can view existing waypoints, routes, or tracks on the graphic map, or create new waypoints or routes. There are both water-based (blue water) and land-based (topography) charts available. If you want to be safe and secure in remote wilderness areas, especially if you like to explore areas off of marked trails, a map GPS unit is a very worthwhile expense.

- Consider buying a small weather radio so you can keep informed of local weather forecasts. Some are even programmed to sound an alarm if inclement weather is approaching. Lightning kills more people in Florida than in any other state; always seek shelter if you are caught in a lightning storm.

- Bring a dependable waterproof flashlight, regardless of whether or not you plan on paddling after dark. Experienced canoeists and kayakers always expect the unexpected, so if you should unexpectedly find yourself out after dark, you will be thankful you have a light.

- Always bring an extra paddle and strap it to one of the thwarts so it will remain with the canoe in case you capsize. Also, always keep a small anchor with at least 20 feet of rope tied to either the bow or stern. Keep the rope loose so that if you capsize in a strong tidal flow, the anchor will automatically descend and keep your canoe from drifting away faster than you can swim. If you are near the mouth of one of the rivers and the tide is going out, your canoe could end up taking a solo journey into the Gulf of Mexico. To watch your canoe get farther and farther away on its way into the Gulf can be a bit disheartening to say the least.

- *Always* wear a life vest, especially if you are solo. (It is required to have on board a U.S. Coast Guard–approved life vest.) If you think that conventional life vests are too hot or cumbersome, consider using a belt-type life preserver. These have an inflatable bag attached to the belt. The bag is inflated by pulling a handle that activates a compressed-air cylinder (pray that it works!). A good life vest with pockets, however, is convenient, because it gives you a place to keep important items on your person, such as your car keys.

- *Never* wear heavy pants (like jeans) or hiking boots when canoeing. If you capsize you will be weighted down, and drowning might become a very real possibility.

- If you do capsize in a canoe, *do not panic* (you have a life vest on, right?). Flip it back upright and climb back in. You can paddle a canoe even if it's full of water, so paddle toward shore or shallow water as best you can. Once you are in a safe situation, bail out the water and then go recover any gear that may have drifted away.

- Tie your important gear to the canoe thwarts or consider using a mesh cargo net made of bungee cord that is specifically designed to protect your gear from being lost if you capsize. The mesh net attaches to the thwarts and gunwales with plastic hooks and typically covers about 6 feet of gear in a canoe.

- When camping on chickees (elevated wood docks with a roof) that are near the Gulf of Mexico, be sure to secure your canoe with enough rope to allow your canoe to float up and down with the tide (learn the bowline knot). Tides that occur on or near the new moon or full moon (spring tides) will have higher highs and lower lows than tides that occur around the quarter-moon phases (neap tides). There is about a 4 to 6 foot height difference between tides at chickees located near river mouths that flow into the Gulf of Mexico. Experience has taught me to bring along a pair of small blocks-and-tackle. Tie one to the overhead beam on each side of the chickee, loop a rope through them to the bow and stern of the canoe, remove any heavy gear, then simply pull the canoe up until it is suspended safely above the high-tide line. Also, always pull your canoe completely out of the water above the high-tide line when at land-based campsites, especially on beaches where tidal flow can be strong.

- Because full-moon and new-moon tides are higher and lower than average levels, this translates to much stronger tidal flows in between highs and lows, which can make paddling against them difficult. If tides are too strong, simply wait until they subside.

- If you are paddling in a following tide (flowing the same direction you are traveling) and you are in a river near the Gulf of Mexico where tides can be very strong, be sure to stay out in the open water and not near tree-lined shores. If your canoe hits a low-lying branch with a strong following tide, it can turn your canoe sideways and cause you to capsize.

- One of the best items you can bring along with you when canoeing and camping in the Everglades backcountry is a folding chair. On solo trips I prefer to place a low, aluminum-frame beach chair in front of the rear seat. This allows you to paddle while sitting in a chair with a back, and you also have a chair to sit in at your campsite. This is a definite plus! Consider attaching fishing-rod holders to the chair by drilling through the back frame and using galvanized or stainless-steel bolts to secure them firmly. This allows you to troll for fish while paddling between campsites and also offers a convenient place to keep your fishing rods when they're not in use. When trolling use a floating lure with a lip (Mirro-Lure, Rapala, Yo-Zuri) that causes it to dive underwater with a swimming motion while you're paddling the canoe, but that floats to the surface when stopped. Just remember to reel it in when you enter winding creeks so the hooks won't snag underwater roots when rounding bends, and watch for low branches if a rod is in the holder.

- Keep all of your clothes, sleeping bag, blankets, etc., in waterproof duffel bags. These are available in a variety of sizes from sporting-goods outlets.

- A push pole is convenient to have aboard a canoe, and these work especially well for keeping a canoe in place without having to throw out an anchor. Secure a loop of rope at either the bow or stern (stern if you are solo) then run the push pole through the loop and into the mud bottom. Commercial push poles come in a variety of lengths and consist of a hollow fiberglass pole with a pointed metal tip on one end and a metal V on the other end, which allows for poling boats in shallow water. A push pole 8 to 10 feet in length is adequate for a canoe.

- Don't just pack a bunch of food. Plan day-to-day meals (with enough for one extra day just in case) and pack them accordingly. Avoid canned and bottled goods as much as possible so as not to generate too much trash. There are no trash receptacles at any of the Everglades National Park backcountry campsites, so you are required to bring your trash out with you. The best food items to bring along are fresh fruits and vegetables that do not require refrigeration. Consider such items as white potatoes, sweet potatoes, corn on the cob, asparagus, brussel sprouts, squash (summer and winter), beets, citrus, and anything else that meets your fancy. Remove everything from its grocery-store packaging, wash it, dry it, and repack it in large, sealable plastic bags (store it out of the sun). This way you are lightening your load with each meal and not generating trash in the process. Nuts, cereal, and health bars are good for snacks. Use apple juice instead of milk for your morning cereal because it doesn't require refrigeration, or use powdered milk.

- Bring plastic gallon jugs of water—at least one gallon per day per person. Once your canoe is packed, simply toss the gallon jugs around wherever they will fit, but secure a few of them to a thwart in case you capsize. Gallon jugs are much more convenient than any other size, and you can squash them after they're empty so they don't take up too much room.

- If you are a coffee drinker, buy a stainless-steel coffee press. These are great for camping because you simply put the coffee grounds in the press, pour in boiling water, and, when it's been in the press five minutes or so, insert the metal filter plunger and push it down to separate the water from the grounds. Voila! Fresh-brewed coffee with no muss or fuss. I learned this from my wife. Thank you, honey!

- Because many of the backcountry campsites are elevated wood chickees, you will need to bring a cook stove (propane or pressurized fuel) or a charcoal grill. Some grills have vents at the bottom—be sure they're closed to ensure that hot embers do not fall on the chickee (setting fire to your chickee would be very bad!). Remember too that campfires are banned at all campsites in Everglades National Park except on designated beaches (see the Prohibited and Restricted Activities section on pages 22–24).

- Quick-drying clothes are a good choice for canoeing in southern Florida, both in summer and winter. My favorite canoeing pants are lightweight cotton pajama bottoms. They dry quickly, slip on and off with ease, keep the sun off your legs, and are inexpensive. They won't weigh you down if you capsize, either. Nylon pants and shorts (or pants with zippered legs that can be removed to create shorts) are excellent too, but rayon is hot. Extra-large baggy white cotton shirts are also a plus, along with a wide-brimmed hat and sunscreen.

Inside Everglades National Park

Flamingo Lodge, Marina & Outpost Resort
Located at Flamingo
(239) 695–3101, ext. 355
www.flamingolodge.com

- Canoe and kayak rentals
- Fishing skiff rentals
- Shuttle service (canoes and kayaks only; no passengers)

Everglades National Park Boat Tours
Located at the Gulf Coast Ranger Station in Everglades City
(239) 695–2591 or (800) 445–7724 (Florida only)
www.evergladesnatlboatours.com

- Canoe rentals
- Shuttle service (drop-off/pick-up; transportation back from Flamingo for those paddling the entire Wilderness Waterway)

  Note: The contract to operate boat tours, canoe and kayak rentals, and a gift shop at Everglades City was awarded to Guest Services, a Fairfax, Virginia, company, in May 2004. Everglades National Park Boat Tours is planning to take legal action against the National Park Service, so the situation is unresolved as this guide goes to press. Contact the Gulf Coast Visitor Center at (239) 695–3311 if the above telephone numbers are no longer in operation.

Outside Everglades National Park

Everglades Hostel & Tours
Located in Florida City
(305) 248–1122 or (800) 372–3874
www.evergladeshostel.com

- canoe rentals
- bike rentals

Florida Bay Outfitters
Located at Mile Marker 104 on Key Largo
(305) 451–3018
www.kayakfloridakeys.com

- canoe and kayak rentals

Glades Haven
Located in Everglades City
(239) 695–2579
www.gladeshaven.com

- canoe and kayak rentals
- fishing-skiff rentals
- pontoon-boat rentals

Ivey House & North American Canoe Tours
Located in Everglades City
(239) 695–3299
www.iveyhouse.com

- canoe and kayak rentals
- camping-gear rentals
- shuttle service (drop-off/pick-up; vehicle delivery from Everglades City to Flamingo for those paddling the entire Wilderness Waterway, then pick up your keys from the Flamingo dock master when you arrive)
- guided day trips and overnight tours

Outdoor Resorts
Located in Everglades City
(239) 695–2881

- canoe and kayak rentals
- fishing-skiff rentals
- shuttle service (transportation back from Flamingo for those paddling the entire Wilderness Waterway)

The following list of gear is offered to ensure that you haven't forgotten any important items.

General

- ☐ U.S. Coast Guard–approved life vest required
- ☐ Whistle (required in canoes and kayaks; keep it on a lanyard around your neck or in a pocket on your life vest if it has one)
- ☐ Paddles (with at least one spare)
- ☐ Small anchor (with at least 20 feet of line)
- ☐ Small bucket for bailing (large sponges are excellent, too)
- ☐ Bow and stern lines (at least 20 feet each)
- ☐ Waterproof duffel bags and dry boxes for clothing and sleeping bags
- ☐ Flares
- ☐ Red flag for hailing boaters in case of an emergency
- ☐ Aerosol air horn (three blasts is the international distress signal)
- ☐ Small fire extinguisher
- ☐ Battery-powered light for navigating at night
- ☐ Two small blocks-and-tackle (optional, but an easy way to hoist your canoe out of the water at chickees instead of worrying about tides all night)
- ☐ Assorted bungee cords to secure gear
- ☐ Waterproof tarp to cover the canoe (keeps gear and the canoe dry in case of rain, even while paddling)

Navigation

- ☐ Nautical charts (Rather than purchasing waterproof charts, I find it best to buy NOAA charts, cut them into sections, and then have the sections laminated. I mark them so I know which side connects to the next, and I use a grease pencil to mark my route. These are much easier to handle while paddling than an entire chart.)
- ☐ Compass (keep it on the lanyard with your whistle)
- ☐ Tide chart
- ☐ Binoculars (to look for markers as well as wildlife)
- ☐ Hand-held GPS (optional, but a good idea)

Permits and Regulations

- ☐ Backcountry (wilderness) camping permit
- ☐ Float plan (with an emergency contact)

- ☐ Wilderness regulations
- ☐ Fishing license and regulations
- ☐ Vessel registration (required even for a canoe if powered by an outboard motor)

Shelter

- ☐ Tent with no-see-um netting (tents must be freestanding for chickees)
- ☐ Rain fly for tent
- ☐ Light sleeping bag (clothing bags and life vests make good pillows)
- ☐ Sleeping pad for comfort (some are self-inflating)
- ☐ Tarp with supports for camping on beaches (shade)
- ☐ Waterproof ground tarp (slightly smaller than the bottom of the tent so rain does not collect on it)

Water and Food

- ☐ Water—one gallon per person per day (fresh water is not available in the backcountry)
- ☐ Water-purifying tablets
- ☐ Powdered Gatorade
- ☐ Food—with an extra day's supply (fresh fruits and vegetables help cut down on cans and bottles; there are no trash receptacles in the backcountry)
- ☐ Health or energy bars
- ☐ Raccoon-proof storage—not Styrofoam—for food and water

Cooking

- ☐ Portable stove or grill (consider propane stoves; there is a single burner available that screws directly onto the propane cylinder, but they are a little tippy without support)
- ☐ Fuel/charcoal (consider self-lighting charcoal to avoid carrying fuel)
- ☐ Waterproof matches or butane lighters
- ☐ Cooking gear and utensils (no disposable plastic)
- ☐ Aluminum foil (wrap a potato in it and toss it in the coals)
- ☐ Paper towels for cleaning and starting fires
- ☐ Biodegradable soap with sponge

Clothing

- ☐ Rain gear
- ☐ Cold- or warm-weather clothes (depending on time of year, of course)
- ☐ Lightweight long-sleeve shirt and pants for sun and bug protection (light cotton pajama bottoms are good, inexpensive paddling pants)

- ☐ Hiking sandals (Teva-style) or elastic water socks
- ☐ Wide-brimmed hat
- ☐ Bathing suit (optional!)

Personal Gear

- ☐ First-aid kit (with sting-relief swabs for bee and wasp stings and pain-relief antibiotic ointment for cuts as well as stab wounds from stingrays or cat-fish if you are an angler)
- ☐ Knife (holstered fish filet knives are excellent)
- ☐ Waterproof flashlight with spare bulb and batteries
- ☐ Hatchet or, better yet, a limb saw to cut up dead wood for campfires (on beaches only in Everglades National Park)
- ☐ Wristwatch for calculating tides
- ☐ Sunglasses (polarized with brown lenses are best for the Everglades)
- ☐ Waterproof sunscreen (SPF 30 or higher)
- ☐ Camera and film (disposable waterproof cameras are excellent for prints; if you bring an expensive camera be sure to pack it in a watertight container)
- ☐ Mask, snorkel, fins, and dive flag (few diving opportunities exist in Everglades National Park due to murky water, but fins may come in handy if you flip your canoe)
- ☐ Insect repellent (20 to 30 percent DEET is sufficient)
- ☐ Portable weather radio
- ☐ Handheld VHF marine radio (optional, but a good idea)
- ☐ Cellular phone (some may not work in the Everglades backcountry)
- ☐ Battery-powered light for inside tent (bring a good book)
- ☐ Folding chair (short aluminum-frame beach chairs are excellent)
- ☐ Hammock (optional, but great for relaxing or napping at chickees)
- ☐ Fishing tackle and gear
- ☐ Personal hygiene items
- ☐ Prescription medicine (allergy pills if you need them)
- ☐ Biodegradable toilet tissue
- ☐ Trowel for digging a toilet hole at land-based campsites
- ☐ Trash bags

Before packing spread all of your gear out on the floor and go over each item (how necessary is it?). Always pack all of your gear in your canoe (or kayak) at home to see how (or even *if*) everything fits. Keep items together that you may need frequently, and pack them close to your seat for easy access. It always seems like a lot of gear, but do not skimp on safety equipment if you need to downsize. From my experience a 17-foot Grumman aluminum canoe will be fully loaded when packed with gear, food, and water for a ten-day solo trip along the Wilderness Waterway in Everglades National Park. Have fun!

(in alphabetical order)

Campsite Name	Type of Site	Toilet	Table	Dock
Broad River	Ground	✓	✓	✓
Camp Lonesome	Ground	✓	✓	✓
Canepatch	Ground	✓	✓	✓
Cape Sable	Beach	☐	☐	☐
Clubhouse Beach	Beach	☐	☐	☐
Darwin's Place	Ground	✓	✓	☐
East Clubhouse Beach	Beach	☐	☐	☐
Graveyard Creek	Ground	✓	✓	✓
Harney River	Single chickee	✓	☐	✓
Hells Bay	Double chickee	✓	☐	✓
Highland Beach	Beach	☐	☐	☐
Hog Key	Single chickee	☐	☐	✓
Joe River	Double chickee	✓	☐	✓
Kingston Key	Double chickee	✓	☐	✓
Lane Bay	Single chickee	✓	☐	✓
Lard Can	Ground	✓	☐	☐
Lopez River	Ground	✓	✓	☐
Lostmans Five	Ground	✓	☐	✓
Mormon Key	Beach	☐	☐	☐
New Turkey Key	Beach	✓	☐	☐
North River	Single chickee	✓	☐	✓
Oyster Bay	Double chickee	✓	☐	✓
Pavilion Key	Beach	✓	☐	☐
Pearl Bay	Double chickee	✓	☐	✓
Picnic Key	Beach	✓	☐	✓
Plate Creek	Double chickee	✓	☐	✓

Campsite Name	Type of Site	Toilet	Table	Dock
Rabbit Key	Beach	✓	☐	☐
Roberts River	Double chickee	✓	☐	✓
Rodgers River	Double chickee	✓	☐	✓
Shark Point	Ground	☐	☐	☐
South Joe River	Double chickee	✓	☐	✓
Sunday Bay	Double chickee	✓	☐	✓
Sweetwater	Double chickee	✓	☐	✓
Tiger Key	Beach	☐	☐	☐
Turkey Key	Beach	☐	☐	☐
Watson's Place	Ground	✓	✓	✓
Watson River	Single chickee	✓	✓	✓
Willy Willy	Ground	✓	☐	✓

Note: Some of the above campsites are not generally associated with the Wilderness Waterway but are accessible from it.

Appendix G
Conservation Organizations

The conservation organizations listed below offer guided field trips into wilderness areas of South Florida. Contact them for schedules of upcoming events.

Fairchild Tropical Botanic Garden
10901 Old Cutler Road
Coral Gables, FL 33156
(305) 667–1651
www.fairchildgarden.org

Florida Native Plant Society—Dade Chapter
Monthly meetings: third Tuesday of each month; 7:30 P.M.
Fairchild Tropical Botanic Garden
10901 Old Cutler Road
Coral Gables, FL 33156

Florida Trail Association
5415 Southwest 13 Street
Gainesville, FL 32608
(877) HIKE–FLA (445–3352)
E-mail: fta@florida-trail.org
www.florida-trail.org

Florida Trail Association—Alligator Amblers Chapter
Serves Charlotte, Collier, and Lee Counties
Monthly meetings: second Thursday of each month; 7:00 P.M.
Various locations
http://amblers.florida-trail.org

Florida Trail Association—Big Cypress Chapter
Serves Miami-Dade and Monroe Counties
Monthly meetings: third Thursday of each month; 7:30 P.M.
Palmetto Senior High School
7351 Southwest 128 Street
Pinecrest, FL 33156
http://cypress.florida-trail.org

North American Butterfly Association—Miami Blue Chapter
Monthly meetings: first Sunday of each month; 1:00 P.M.
Castellow Hammock Park
22301 Southwest 162 Avenue
Redland, FL 33170
(305) 242–7688 (for information or to confirm meeting date and time)
E-mail: naba@naba.org

Sierra Club—Miami Group
Monthly meetings: second Monday of each month; 7:00 P.M.
Coral Gables Women's Club
1001 East Ponce de Leon Boulevard
Coral Gables, FL 33134
Hotline: (305) 667–7311
www.sierraclub.org/chapters/fl/miami

Tropical Audubon Society
5530 Sunset Drive
Miami, FL 33143
(305) 666–5111
www.tropicalaudubon.org

Index

About the Author

Roger L. Hammer is a native Floridian who has explored the Everglades region extensively for more than thirty years. He is a senior interpretive naturalist for the Miami-Dade Parks Department and director of Castellow Hammock Nature Center. He is also an active volunteer, class instructor, and field-trip leader for Fairchild Tropical Botanic Garden and a member of the board of directors of Tropical Audubon Society. He has received awards for conservation and education from the Florida Native Plant Society, TREEmendous Miami, and Tropical Audubon Society. He is also the author of *Everglades Wildflowers* (The Globe Pequot Press, 2002) and *Florida Keys Wildflowers* (The Globe Pequot Press, 2004). His hobbies include canoeing, kayaking, fishing, camping, gardening, and wildflower photography.